Trusting God
through Tears

I have watched Jehu and his family walk the path of deepest pain. In this book Jehu presents his honest emotions and thoughts regarding the death of his son, but we can also see him emerge triumphant in his faith. I highly recommend that every grieving parent read this book.

Marilyn Willett Heavilin
author of *Roses in December*

As a father of two sons killed in an automobile accident and a grieving and at times bewildered parent, this book helped me to gain a clearer concept on trusting the wisdom of God in the results which He allows in our lives. On a number of occasions as I read, I found myself saying, "Yes, Lord, You are God and I must trust You."

Pastor Ed Lasko
Middletown Baptist Church

TRUSTING GOD
through TEARS

A Story to Encourage

Jehu Thomas Burton

Foreword by Dan Allender

Baker Books

A Division of Baker Book House Co
Grand Rapids, Michigan 49516

Published by Baker Books
a division of Baker Book House Company
P.O. Box 6287, Grand Rapids, MI 49516-6287

Printed in the United States of America

Library of Congress Cataloging-in-Publication Data

Burton, Jehu Thomas, 1950–
      Trusting God through tears : a story to encourage / Jehu Thomas
   Burton.
         p.   cm.
      ISBN 0-8010-6161-X (pbk.)
         1. Consolation. 2. Children—Death—Religious aspects—
      Christianity. 3. Bereavement—Religious aspects—Christianity.
      4. Grief—Religious aspects—Christianity. 5. Burton, Jehu Thomas,
      1950–   I. Title.
      BV4907B83   2000
      248.8'66—dc21   99-086399

All Scripture quotations are from the HOLY BIBLE, NEW INTERNATIONAL VERSION®. NIV®. Copyright © 1973, 1978, 1984 by International Bible Society. Used by permission of Zondervan Publishing House. All rights reserved.

"Home Free" by Wayne Watson on page 65 is ©1990 Word Music, Inc. (ASCAP), 65 Music Square West, Nashville, TN 37203/Material Music (Admin. by Word Music, Inc.) (ASCAP), 65 Music Square West, Nashville, TN 37203. All rights reserved. Made in the U.S.A. International copyright secured. Used by permission.

"I Want to Be Where You Are" on page 118 is by Don Moen. ©1989 Integrity's Hosanna! Music/ASCAP. All rights reserved. International copyright secured. Used by permission.

"True Love" by David Ruis on page 148 is ©1994 Mercy/Vineyard Publishing. All rights reserved. Used by permission.

For current information about all new releases from Baker Book House, visit our web site:
                           http://www.bakerbooks.com

To my precious helpmate, that person chosen by God as my lifetime partner. We have endured life's greatest tragedy and have been shaped and molded into one by God's conforming hand.

Contents

Foreword

The sun was peeking from behind a dark mass of clouds. There are few moments like this in November, and I was determined to find the sunniest spot in the house to read. As it turned out, that spot was my son's bedroom. He was sleeping, so I sat down in his oversized chair, put my feet on his desk, and opened up Jehu's manuscript.

My friend Tremper Longman III had asked me to look at a book that had come to his attention. The only thing I knew about the book was that it chronicled the process of grieving after a death in the Burton family. I was reluctant to read. As a therapist, I deal daily with heartache and loss, and I was not excited about reading a book that would ask me to confront the dark realities of living in a fallen world.

As I read, I felt the tears that were woven into the words and the heartache that beat with each page. I could not keep my eyes off my sleeping son; I could see the slight rise and fall of the covers as he breathed. My son too is twelve. He is a delight to my heart, and I would easily and reflexively give my life for his. My twelve-year-old breathes and Jehu's twelve-year-old son is in the grave. The juxtaposition of our two stories made the reading both compelling and demanding. Life is not fair. God gives and takes according to His pleasure and His purposes. How are we to bear His apparent inequity?

My son turned in bed, and his eyes blinked to my presence. He smiled and turned over to resume the pleasure of sleep. God calls me to live in the midst of both gratitude and sorrow—gratitude for His gifts and ultimately for the grace of His Son, and sorrow for the losses of living in an alien land that is still far from the home we desire.

The haunting call of this book is: How do we face the goodness of God and the offer of His heart to us as we experience suffering that He could unquestionably alter? Jehu offers neither sentimental nor easy palliatives—his grief and the harm to his family is immense. Yet, his story bears the unmistakable mark of God's presence that seizes the reader and takes us not only into the profoundly personal realm of grief but also into the incomprehensible dominion of redemption.

We may never be called to lose a child. But each of us is called to enter more deeply into the reality of living in a fallen world. Far more, if we enter even the fringe of sorrow, we will be invited to taste the odd, wild, transforming pleasure of God's presence, which does not eradicate sorrow but instead throws us deeper into the mystery of His passion for us.

Jehu Burton invites you to walk with him on a journey that allows you to feel his tears and to hear the ultimate mockery of evil—not even death can steal from you faith, hope, and love. This story will take you deeper into the heart of the Father's sacrifice of His Son for your sake. Read with keen hope and rich tears. The journey will change your life.

Dan B. Allender

Preface

In 1991 my son Kelly died, and I began a journey. For the next few years I wrestled with God, trying to understand why He would ever let such a tragic event occur. Why would a loving God let my dreams be crushed?

One day almost three years after Kelly died, I was sitting in my office at work meditating when it just came over me: *I'm going to write a book.* I had had no prior thoughts or plans to write. So I turned to my PC and started typing. I typed the first thirty pages without my fingers leaving the keyboard. I began to realize all that God had taught me over the last three years as I sought answers and tried to understand why God's people suffer. I continued to write over the next year.

The spring of the following year I was in Denver, Colorado, on a business trip. While I was waiting at the airport gate for my return flight, I thought I recognized the person sitting across the aisle from me. I thought it was Dr. Tremper Longman, who had been at our church several months earlier for a conference, but I was not sure. As he began to pack up his belongings to board the plane, I noticed the cover of the manuscript he was reading: *Zechariah*. I remembered Dr. Longman being an Old Testament scholar, so this convinced me that it was he. Approaching him I introduced myself. We traded stories as to why we were in Denver. Tremper told me he had visited a publisher in the Denver area concerning a new manuscript, which prompted me to share with him that I too was writing a book. Tremper asked me what the subject was; I told him it was about my son's death and all that God has taught me as a result. Tremper volunteered to read my manuscript and offer me his opinion. Upon returning home I sent him my manuscript and our friendship began. Tremper later shared with me that he seldom offers to read others' manuscripts. He encouraged me to continue writing, which I did over the next two years.

It was now the spring of 1997, and I had gotten to the point where I wanted to know if my manuscript had any merit. The writing had certainly been therapeutic for me and was a worthy legacy for my remaining children, but I wondered whether it had potential benefit for others. I arranged a lunch meeting in Philadelphia with Tremper to discuss my manuscript. I told him I felt I was to a point where I could get a reasonable assessment from potential publishers. Tremper agreed and suggested that he write a letter of introduction to several publishers he knew. He did so, and in April of 1997 we sent out my manuscript with the letter of introduction to four Christian publishers. I began praying, "Lord, I am giving this manuscript to You; if it is Your pleasure, open the door of Your choosing." Over the next months I received three letters of no interest, but I did not hear from the fourth publisher. I continued praying, relying on God to open the doors. I waited patiently. Fifteen months later I received a letter of interest from Baker Book House. Discussions continued with them, resulting in a book contract and the publishing of this story.

As I reflect back over the eight-year process, it is ever so evident to me of God working out His plan, not mine. It was the Holy Spirit's prompting to start writing. Why else would it have been so spontaneous? What are the odds of my meeting Tremper in the Denver airport and taking the same flight? I see no way that my manuscript would have been published without Tremper's involvement and encouragement. Again, I can only see this as God's direct intervention.

I am further convinced it was God's timing that controlled the publisher's response. There is a reason I waited fifteen months to hear back from Baker. Most likely this was necessary to prepare me for the editing process. It is also obvious that we are frequently unable to see God's intervention at the moment. It is only after the fact that the pieces of the puzzle begin to fit together, and we see God's hand executing the impossible. His timing and the wisdom of His plan far exceed our best plans.

God is in control of our lives. Not just the big events but the small everyday events as well. Can we trust Him with that tremendous power over our lives? This book is one person's testimony of that trust, and it is my desire to share with you what God has taught me.

I wish to thank those who have encouraged me along the way and made this book a reality. Thanks to Marilyn Heavilin who saw the book within me and encouraged me to keep writing. Thanks to Jim Powell and Ed Lasko for offering their comments and support. Thanks to Tremper Longman for being my champion and opening the door to my publisher. Thanks to Paul Engle for seeing that this book was published. Thanks to Sharon Van Houten for capturing my vision and transforming my manuscript into a readable book.

Introduction

Most of my life I have avoided suffering, doing everything within my power to dissociate myself from it. Similarly, I have believed the evidence of God's blessing was a life free from suffering. However, I now view suffering from a completely opposite perspective. I believe that the individuals truly blessed of God are those of us who experience the fiery crucible of pain, tribulation, and trials, for it is during these times we are drawn closest to God. I can now see how God uses suffering as His most effective tool for changing everything about the way we live and how we treat other people. God's conforming hand is most active in our life in the midst of tribulation.

I have experienced a life-changing event—one that has altered my nature, my view of life, my life's priorities, and my relationship with every person I shall meet for the rest of my life. God used the death of my son to change me, and these changes are the fruit born out of my suffering.

On February 19, 1991, my wife, Patty, found our twelve-year-old son, Kelly, dead in his bed from a cerebral hemorrhage. My world collapsed. Everything I once valued now seemed worthless. All my goals for life now seemed meaningless. As time wore on I was driven deeper and deeper toward the bottom of the pit. The days grew darker and darker. The agony became suffocating and inescapable. My dreams for life were destroyed. My ideal family was now a statistic. My plans for tomorrow would never be realized. Life itself became difficult. Getting out of bed in the morning became a major task.

Once you arrive at the bottom of the pit, you have two choices. One, you can arise in anger and rebellion against God, blaming Him for everything wrong in your life and pointing to Him as the source of all your disappointments. Or, two, you can submit to God's authority over you and seek His comfort and direction in your life.

I believe God led me to choose the latter path, for I was humbled before Him. I became a broken man and ultimately submitted to His authority over my family and me.

I realized I really had no control over anything. I could not bring my son back to life. I could not restore my dreams. I could not remove my wife's grief or even my own. I could not turn back time. I could not replace sadness with happiness. It was as if I was traveling down a steep hill in an automobile with no brakes and no steering wheel, totally dependent on the whimsical motion of the car.

Drained of all sense of self-sufficiency, I felt incapable of accomplishing even the simplest task. All feelings of independence and pride in self were shattered. I was forced to look to God moment by moment seeking His direction and assistance to make it through each day.

In the following months I yielded each day to Jesus Christ, asking Him, "Where is it, Lord, that You want me to go, and what is it that You want me to do today?" He began to show me things I had not seen before. Scripture passages that previously had little impact on me were now illumined and offered comfort and explanation for what I was experiencing. My perspective was changing: I realized I was clay in the potter's hands, and I was now able to say, "Lord, you are in control; make me and shape me as You will."

Every ounce of my body not previously given to the Lord was now His. Nothing was left that was my own. I accepted His complete dominion over me and all that happened in my life: Everything good was the result of His blessing, and everything bad had passed through His hands and been permitted.

After Kelly died, I began to taste the bitterness of suffering. At first, as most would do, I fought the pain and resisted the truth God wanted to teach me, but in time, I succumbed to His persistence. I had lived forty years successfully avoiding significant personal suffering and failing to be influenced to a large degree by others' suffering. My time had come. God was now going to change me. Slowly, I began to see how God uses suffering to conform us in His image. It is during times of trial that we most frequently seek the Lord's direction; it is during tribulation that God has our attention. So I have become convinced in the fire of suffering we are most malleable in God's hands. Even as Christians, when we are not in a broken state we have a latent desire to control our destiny. However, when we are broken and contrite in spirit we are most apt to submit to the Lord's direction and leading.

Through my experience I have come to the point where I believe God uses suffering as His most effective tool to conform us in His image. Sometimes He originates the suffering and other times He uses the product of Satan's work. Regardless of the source of suffering, God is able to produce fruit, if we submit to rather than rebel against His authority. It does not matter if God initiated the suffering for discipline purposes or if Satan invoked the hardship. God is able to use it all to accomplish His overriding purposes. The fruit may not always be obvious as it is manifested in our conformance to the image of Christ. This conforming process may be so gradual we have difficulty recognizing it. Further fruit is born when God influences others through our response to His conformance. As I read the writings of the apostle Paul I am further convinced of this truth. Again and again, he admonishes us not to be surprised when confronted with suffering. All believers must accept suffering as an attribute of the Christian faith. God uses it to change us into the people He wants us to be.

I believe the Holy Spirit speaks to individual hearts and reveals to us God's truth as we read and meditate on His Word. I also believe it then becomes our responsibility to share with others what the Holy Spirit has revealed to us. Proverbs 27:17 states, "As iron sharpens iron, so one man sharpens another." We are to "sharpen" one another through the teachings of the Holy Spirit. Therefore, I have attempted in this writing to let you look into a broken heart, to see the depths of the wound and examine the damage, knowing the Holy Spirit will then be free to use it as He wills to change and teach you as He pleases.

Few parents experience the death of their young child, and you need not experience it personally to learn from God's teaching. God has not ordained that we all undergo the same trials; nor does He teach each one of us the same lessons. Therefore, I believe I am to share what the Lord has taught me so others may learn from these lessons.

I have come to the point where I need not know if God took my son or if Satan or sin caused his death. Regardless of who or what is responsible, I can see how God has used Kelly's death in many ways for His purposes. This is the fruit God has produced from my loss. I am comforted to know my son's death is not in vain and God is able to create good from human tragedy.

The prayers that precede each chapter are recorded conversations with my Lord that occurred throughout the summer of 1991 as I made repeated business trips following my son's death. During those moments in the crowded plane at 30,000 feet as I gazed out the window at the floating clouds, it was as if I was free of earth's encumbrances, suspended between earthly thoughts and the heavenly realm. I was free to focus on my Lord and my life.

In the following chapters I seek to accomplish the following objectives:

1. Establish credibility with you the reader by answering the question, "Why do I have the right to address the subject of suffering?"
2. Share what God has taught me regarding suffering so that you might embrace a new view of suffering and how God uses it for His purposes.
3. Encourage you to trust God in all situations—even the most severe trial.

Kelly Thomas Burton
June 4, 1978–
February 19, 1991

Oh, dear Lord, where is heaven?

Beyond the eyes of the largest telescope?

At the farthest edge of the universe?

Or, dear Lord, is it just beyond my reach?

Invisible, transparent, floating somewhere just beyond earth's atmosphere?

Can my hand pass through it undisturbed?

Will I have form there?

Will I know and recognize my loved ones?

Will my friendships continue?

Will I feel reunited and whole again?

Or, dear Lord, will all of this seem meaningless and will I only seek the
warmth of Your love?

Chapter 1

Death Invades

It was the middle of February, and we had taken a weekend retreat to my brother-in-law Tommy's home in Clarion, Pennsylvania. Shane, our older son who had just turned sixteen, did not go with us and stayed with one of his friends. Our other two children, twelve-year-old Kelly and nine-year-old Bethany, made the trip with my wife and me. We were in the prime of family life.

Clarion is in a rural area northeast of Pittsburgh. Tommy and his family live next to Cooks Forest State Park, which is 2,000 acres of virgin timber—mostly tall pines that have seen the test of time. There was fresh snow that Saturday morning, and the two families elected to go sledding. We all went, including Tommy's three younger children. What a joyous time it was. I felt like a young boy again, jumping up off the sled after a great ride, performing a celebration dance as I screamed out with excitement. I shall never forget the moment on that mountaintop as the snow continued to fall; it was so peaceful and quiet. There was no sound except the occasional chatter of a blue jay, the intermittent laughter of the children, and the sound of air rushing through my nostrils. Huge snowflakes were falling as I gazed across the valley surrounded by large pines draped in fresh-fallen snow. This was an exceptional moment. None like I could ever remember experiencing. I was at peace with my world and felt so secure and happy. Life was so good! I felt so alive! I was reminded how blessed I was to have a lovely wife, three healthy children, and a successful career. God had indeed been gracious. I stood there for a few brief seconds, appreciating the glorious feeling of contentment and joy. This moment was the pinnacle of my life. Never again would it all fit together as it did that day.

We returned home to Elkton, Maryland, on Sunday and started a routine week on Monday. However, things began to deteriorate Monday afternoon. I began to feel nauseous as typical flu symptoms began to emerge. I left work early to return home, finding Bethany and Kelly also showing the same symptoms. Kelly's symptoms were a bit more violent, but we were confident that a good night's sleep would help us all feel better in the morning. How blinded we were to the reality of what was happening.

In God's providence, we all stayed home the next day. Everyone had aroused by 9:00 A.M. except for Kelly. As my wife, Patty, opened his bedroom door to wake him, I heard the dreadful scream. I rushed to his room to find Kelly's blotchy blue body. I knew the moment I saw him that his spirit was gone. Patty called 911 as I attempted CPR, but I could not even open his mouth. His jaws were locked shut, and his body was already stiff and lifeless. I returned to our bedroom where Patty was still talking to the 911 operator. I took the phone from her and told the operator that my son was dead.

The next moments were sheer pandemonium as Patty ran back to Kelly's room screaming. I have never had such a feeling of helplessness. There was absolutely nothing I could do. Patty ran out of the house and into the front yard, falling to her knees crying. It was a gray, rainy morning. I ran after her and tried to lift her up, but I was too weak. A passing motorist saw us and stopped, wondering what in the world was happening. She parked her car and hurriedly walked up to us. I told her that we had just found our son dead in his bed. She told us that she was a nurse and asked if there was any way she could help. In our dazed state, I am sure we seemed quite unresponsive and had no idea of anything she could do. She offered a brief condolence and left. Patty and I went back inside to be with Kelly.

It was over; no warning; no second chance. The agony and reality of death were upon us. What had happened? How could a young, vibrant boy be alive one moment and dead the next? Why had this happened to us? This was only the beginning of those dreadful "why" questions.

I soon began to realize how little control I had over life. The police arrived, and hours passed as the detectives inspected Kelly and his room with the door shut. There was an interrogation by one of the detectives as I explained all that had transpired. We waited for the medical examiner to arrive. Finally in desperation I asked the detective if we could proceed with removing Kelly's body. He agreed, and the cart was taken upstairs to Kelly's room. With a flood of emotions I said, "This is my son; I'll take care of him." I lifted Kelly's body up off the bed and placed it in the body bag with trembling arms and hands. And then the final act—weeping and trembling, I fumbled to zip up the bag. A tremendous pressure gripped my chest as I gasped for air. That moment is scorched in my mind, never to be forgotten. I did not realize then that I would be faced with a lifetime of replaying that video over and over in my mind.

After Kelly's body was placed in the van, the medical examiner arrived. I recounted for him all the events. I told him how our son had flu symptoms the night before, and I speculated that he either choked on his vomit or a blood vessel had broken in his head. However, there was no sign of vomiting, and he was lying in a peaceful, sleeping position.

We were told that our son's body would be transported to Baltimore for an autopsy, in spite of our severe objections. We made a hasty call to our pediatrician only to have him tell us that we had no choice and that we must comply. This was the first of many hard lessons as I was forced to accept decisions and plans that were different from mine.

After Kelly's body was removed, the critical phone calls had to be made. How do you tell someone your twelve-year-old son has died? How do you gently drop a two-ton weight? There is no way! The shock of those words "Kelly is dead" pierced the morning air from coast to coast as I called our relatives and closest friends.

I called my office to tell my secretary I would not be coming in today nor did I know when I would return. I stumbled to find the right words. There were no right words. I then blurted out we had found our son Kelly dead in his bed.

That evening as the word spread, well-meaning friends began to arrive. I shall never forget the face of one neighbor who had coached Kelly in basketball and whose son was the same age as Kelly. When I greeted him at the front door, he could not speak; his facial muscles trembled; his eyes were wet with tears, and he stumbled to make a sound with his voice. We could only embrace each other and postpone the words for another day.

Two days later we had the confirmation that Kelly had died of a massive cerebral hemorrhage from an A-V malformation. There was an artery or vein deep in the center of his brain that was deformed from birth, and it had failed abruptly. The doctors reassured us there was nothing that could have been done even if we had known what was happening. We were told the symptoms of a cerebral hemorrhage are very similar to that of the flu. It was as if God had disguised what was happening so no human would intervene.

Preparing for the Funeral

Over the next few days, we slid into automatic. We had to decide which clothes Kelly would wear for the funeral, we had to select the casket, pick the songs for the service, choose the burial location, decide if the casket would be open or closed, on and on. These were very difficult decisions that no one plans to make for their child.

Choosing the Clothes

My recollection was most people are buried in their best clothes; that was usually a suit for the man. Kelly did not own a suit. It would not have been his nature to wear a suit. He was a twelve-year-old who felt most comfortable in jeans and sneakers. Patty and I realized without even discussing it that Kelly should be buried in his favorite outfit—the old white turtleneck covered by the favorite T-shirt with a small hole in the chest, blue jeans, Nike sneakers, and the old dirty white University of North Carolina baseball hat. It was not fancy, but it was Kelly.

As we chose the clothing, I recalled the shopping trip to buy his sneakers. It was the beginning of the seventh-grade basketball season. Kelly had finally made the big leagues of organized sports. He was on a real team with uniforms, scheduled practices, games, referees, the whole ball of wax. He was so excited! There was only one place in town to buy these special shoes—"Save on Sneaks," the sports shoe Mecca. Kelly and I gazed over the display of shoes. This was indeed a special moment. One of life's highlights for a twelve-year-old boy. Kelly already knew in his mind the

27

weapon of choice; however, I could see his usual reluctance and apprehension. He was afraid the price was too high. I thought, *Do we go for it? Should I make his day?* We did it! We bought the Nike Air Jordans. He loved those shoes. It was now fitting that he should wear them into eternity.

The Private Viewing

It was now Friday morning. The service was to be that evening, and Patty and I were scheduled to go to the funeral home to see our son for the first time since his death. We invited Patty's sister, Cynth, and brother, Tommy, to go with us for support. As I drove to the funeral home, I was weak and light-headed, wondering if I could even drive there without passing out. I concealed my weakness from the others and tried to be strong. In retrospect, I should have asked Tommy to drive. By God's grace, we arrived safely.

As we entered the room, my eyes immediately went to him as he lay so still in the casket. I slowly walked up to the casket, wondering if it was really him. As I began to look at every detail, I could see the telltale signs of the autopsy. I quietly reassured myself that no one else would notice, because no one would look him over so intently as I.

His face was different. It was no longer the face of a boy but the face of a more mature person. I realized he had grown up in those last moments before his spirit departed. He had come face-to-face with life, the spirit world, and those eternal things that appear only occasionally in our dreams.

We were faced with the question of having the casket open or closed. I recalled someone saying it is better to leave the casket open as it helps people face up to the reality of death. One begins to run through the arguments in your mind—all the reasons to leave the casket open and all the reasons to close it. What do I wish to do? I realized no one had the right to question our decision. Patty and I chose to leave the casket open. Kelly was a beautiful young boy even in death. There was no reason to close the casket, unless we wished to protect others from the stark reality. At that point I had no desire to spare anyone from experiencing a small taste of my agony.

The Writings

One of the officiating pastors asked if we had any writings from Kelly that might be used in the service. We had no recollection of such, but Patty decided to look through his things. To our surprise she found several writings Kelly had done in recent months. These may have been for a school Bible class or may have been written in a private moment. Kelly had chosen two verses of Scripture and had written out what they meant to him. We were amazed at the depth of these two writings.

"He reached down from on high and took hold of me; he drew me out of deep waters" (2 Sam. 22:17). This verse is trying to tell what the Lord does when you believe and trust in him. He will protect you from sin, and especially Satan. You will also get to go to heaven to reign with God.
I love you Lord,

Kelly

"The grace of the Lord Jesus be with God's people. Amen" (Rev. 22:21). This verse is saying that everyone who knows and follows Jesus Christ will be in the grace of our Lord Jesus, the almighty one. For He is great and this is why I trust in Him for He will guide me and help me in troubles I will run into later in this life. Even when I'm not in troubles He is with me. He is the best. I just wish everyone in the world would find Him because He is the best. I love you Lord.

Amen.

Reading these writings helped Patty recall something Kelly had told her several weeks before his death: "I'd rather be in heaven than on this earth." How remarkable was the comment and how unnoticed it was at the moment he spoke it.

I was reminded of Jesus' words in Matthew 18:3: "I tell you the truth, unless you change and become like little children, you will never enter the kingdom of heaven."

At age twelve, Kelly had the faith of which Jesus spoke. He did not question the existence of heaven and, in his young mind, the conclusion was obvious—heaven was a much better place to be than this earth. There was no doubt or question. This is the faith of the little child, believing and never doubting. He accepted it as fact because the Bible said it was so.

Letter from a Friend

Friday morning we received a letter from one of Kelly's friends at school.

Dear Mr. & Mrs. Burton,

I'm so sorry to hear about Kelly's death. Kelly was one of the kindest and nicest friends I've had. He never stabbed you in the back and never talked behind your back. I was able to play soccer in the fall with Kelly. Basketball in the winter was really fun playing along side of a good player like Kelly. Kelly was a different kid in the way that he always was happy, never moody. We are all going to miss Kelly. He was a great friend, classmate, and teammate. I'm going to miss him but I'll never forget him. I'm looking forward to seeing him in heaven. I'm thinking of you and your family in my prayers daily.

Love,
Matthew

I was so touched by this letter. My desire was to somehow include it in the service.

The Service

The service exceeded our every expectation. Over eight hundred people attended. The church was packed and people were turned away. Patty, Shane, Bethany, and I stood next to Kelly's body at the front of the church where we greeted everyone starting at 7:00 P.M. As Matthew and his parents came through the line, I asked Matthew's father if Matthew would be willing to read his letter. He was to give me a sign later if Matthew agreed. The service was scheduled to begin at 8:00, but by 8:30 we were still greeting people and the line was continuing. Our pastor elected to discontinue the greeting, so that the service could begin; he announced we would resume the greeting after the service. Each of us had selected our favorite hymns including one for Kelly, which was "As the Deer." I am reminded of the words we sang. "As the deer panteth for the water, so my soul longeth after Thee. You alone are my heart's desire, and I long to worship Thee."

How beautifully these simple words conveyed the single-minded, passionate relationship we are to have with the Lord Jesus. Was this Kelly's favorite song because he understood and appreciated that kind of relationship with his Savior? I want to believe it was.

Shane had not shown much emotion in the last week, which was not unusual for a sixteen-year-old; however, as the service continued, he began to wail and release all the emotion that had built up. As we grieved openly, our pastor later told us he became uncertain about his ability to deliver his message, because he was overwhelmed by our grief.

We had planned for a time of sharing before our pastor's message. I glanced at Matthew's father and he gave me the "go" sign. My heart was so heavy for Kelly's friends, young children who were forced to deal with grief at such a young age. I had prepared some comments addressed to them. As the sharing time was opened there was a brief period of silence. Who would begin? I stood up and shared my comments, reminding everyone there was a heaven and I would see my son again one day. I encouraged the young people to support one another by being mindful of the glorious place where Kelly now resided. At my conclusion I mentioned the letter and moved toward Matthew. I had no way of knowing he had just told his father he could not read the letter. By the time I got to him he was already in tears. I was prepared to read it if he could not. I passed him the letter and microphone. By God's grace young Matthew was able to read it while sobbing all the way through.

Patty followed with her comments and others shared. What a comfort it was to hear so many people speak of how special Kelly had been in their lives. As parents we have so many desires and goals for our children, and my wife and I were no exception. As I listened, I realized as parents we only see part of our children. As the comments were shared, I was able to see a part of Kelly I had not seen before. Later I remarked to Patty that Kelly had become the child we desired. Through the sharing our pastor was strengthened. He told us later that in seeing Patty and I speak about our son, he received the encouragement he needed to continue.

After the service concluded, we resumed greeting people in the narthex as they departed. Many people remarked at how gracious we were to greet everyone. I had unlimited energy at that point and could have greeted people for hours. God had indeed given us special strength for such an ordeal. Afterward Shane remarked that his chin had become chapped from rubbing on people's shoulders as he was hugged.

That night twenty-six people slept in our house. People were all over the house—on the floor, on couches, any available place. Several neighbors were also kind enough to put family members up for the night. As I walked through the house during the stillness of the night, it was like walking through a disaster shelter. I repeatedly said to myself, "Is this a dream? Oh, Lord, please let this be a dream. May I wake up to find my son alive."

The Burial

I always thought it did not matter where one was buried. I had previously told Patty I did not care where I was buried. But when the moment arrived, I did care. I have always believed the body was nothing more than a shell and once the spirit leaves, the body is as nothing. But now it was different. This body was my Kelly's and it had been created by God, custom made for him. We now had to make a very personal decision of where he would be buried.

My parents had a family plot in Oakhall, Virginia, three hours away, which is where my sister is buried along with other relatives. It was offered and space was available. We could choose one of the local cemeteries, which was unfamiliar to us. I was overcome by a feeling that I did not want my son buried among strangers. How can that be? From where do such feelings come? In the throes of grief one does not always think clearly. Previously well-thought-out plans are subject to change. Positions that were extremely important before can become insignificant. In the midst of our grief we chose the family plot. In retrospect it was the wrong decision. Many times I have longed to visit Kelly's grave, but it was too far away. We have discussed moving him to a nearby place, but that decision is always put off until tomorrow.

We had three pastors participate in the service; however, when I was told none of them was able to officiate at the graveside my mind began to whirl. I quickly concluded I did not want some stranger performing this last earthly act for my son. What were my alternatives? My pastor reassured me he could find a suitable substitute or . . . our minds reached the same point simultaneously. Or . . . I could do it. Yes, I would do it.

Early Saturday morning we assembled the caravan at our house and headed south for the three-hour drive. There was more than enough time to replay how I was going to do this over, and over, and over again in my mind.

As we arrived at the cemetery, the hearse was already in position and a small group of relatives and family friends had gathered. I pulled the car up behind the hearse, leaving enough space to remove the casket. I sat in silence as my eyes scanned the site. It was a cold, brisk February day. I could see the breath of those standing quietly waiting to see my next move. *How can this be? Is it true I am here to bury my son, or is this all a bad dream?* This private moment was interrupted by my mother knocking on the car window saying, "Go speak to your grandmother; she's unable to get out of the car." I returned to reality. This was real. Oh, how very real! After visiting briefly with my grandmother, I returned to the car for a moment to gather my breath.

This was it! It was me, only me. This dreadful ceremony was now solely on my shoulders. I got out of the car and moved toward the hearse, motioning to the other pallbearers. Again, this was my son, and I wanted to participate in each solemn event. I was the first one to reach for the casket handles. I can't even remember what happened to Patty. How did she get from the car to her seat? I was so intent on my responsibilities. We placed the casket in position. Standing beside the hole in the ground, I read Revelation 21:1–7, which speaks of the New Jerusalem. I emphasized the fourth verse: "He will wipe every tear from their eyes. There will be no more death or mourning or crying or pain, for the old order of things has passed away" (Rev. 21:4).

I asked several of my friends to pray, and I concluded. It was over so fast. I did not know what to do next. Was there anything left to do? Do we now just walk away? I moved toward Patty, reaching for her arm and slowly raising her out of the chair. She was limp. She reached to touch Kelly's casket one last time.

The small gathering retired to my father and mother's house. It was quite crowded in the small living room where I stood, but I was all alone. No one knew what to say to me. I was able to occasionally create a small smile when I was approached by a few people. I could already begin to see relief in some people's eyes. For them the solemn event was over; they were eager to return to their normal lives. I was beginning to realize how everyone else would be returning to normal except me. There would be no more "normal" for me.

Here I am, dear Lord, laid prostrate before You. Realizing that I have control over nothing, I am totally dependent on You for everything. All sense of self-sufficiency stripped away, I know that I can only wait for Your next move. Do I live or die, succeed or fail, experience joy or sorrow? These, dear Lord, are Yours to decide.

May 16

Chapter *2*

The Aftermath

Starting to Pick Up the Pieces

In the days and months after Kelly's death there were many repercussions. Shane was fearful of sleeping at home; the memory of his brother's dead body in bed was too vivid and frightening for his young mind and emotions. His coping skills were such that he was not able to deal very well with the trauma. Therefore, he stayed with neighbors or friends at every opportunity. He sought to avoid the subject entirely and frequently became angry when his brother's death was mentioned.

Bethany would cry frequently at school because of something said about Kelly or even some unrelated issue. The teachers were very sensitive and would take Bethany out of the classroom to talk to her and help her get composed. She got to the point of expecting the special attention at school and had to suffer through the readjustment when that attention was no longer given.

Dealing with death is a struggle, and one should not be surprised at the damage it creates. In fact, it would not be normal to cruise through the death of a close family member without seeing a significant impact.

Someone told us about a local grief group for children. It was called K.I.D.D.S.: Kids Involved in Death, Divorce, and Separation. We registered for the next session, which was starting several weeks after Kelly's death. The group met in a local church for eight Wednesday evenings. The leaders divided the children into age groups and used talking, picture drawing, and acting out feelings to get the children to express themselves. The parents met together to talk about the grief process and their children's experiences. The group consisted of about fifteen adults. All were women whose husbands had died, except for one man whose wife had died, and us. Patty and I were the only ones who had lost a child.

The first night Shane and Bethany were excited about finally having a chance to talk to someone their age who had experienced the death of a family member. They could not wait to come back the following week; however, as the meetings went on, Shane and Bethany became less enthused, because it became more difficult for them to express their feelings beyond the initial reaction. We tried to make those evenings special by going out to eat after the meetings. We attempted to keep the dialogue open, mentioning Kelly's name and remembering as many stories as possible. The meetings were profitable for Patty and me as we learned more about grief from the professional counselor who met with the parents; we quickly realized, though, that it was different for us. Having a child die is not the same as having a spouse die. One never expects to bury his or her child. The natural order of things is that parents die first. A child's death seems so unnatural.

Going to church during the first year after Kelly's death was very difficult. I had the vivid image of his casket positioned in the front of the sanctuary. I told myself I was not going to act happy if I was not, and I did not care if that made others uncomfortable. I was not going to pretend life was great, if in fact, it was not. I would sit quietly in church and watch people interact with one another; their laughter and joking made me angry. Why had God permitted my son to die and left so many other families untouched? It all seemed so unfair.

I had never been able to tolerate seeing Patty cry. Previously, I had felt this tremendous responsibility to make her feel better, to alleviate her pain, to correct whatever was wrong. I would do anything to get her to stop crying. When I was unsuccessful in making things better, I would become very frustrated. It was now different. I finally understood the benefits of crying and was able to watch her cry and accept it. I knew her pain and she knew mine. Crying became a tremendous outlet for me too. I actually looked forward to those moments of emotional release.

Out of Control

I had always thought I was in control of my life. Things always seemed to happen the way I wanted them to. Early in my life I decided I wanted to be an engineer. So, by high school, my career was already selected. I went to college and became an engineer. I interviewed prospective employers, selected my best offer, and, upon graduation, had a great job, just as I planned.

I married my high school sweetheart and had three lovely children; I was promoted briskly at work and had a series of challenging assignments. My life was going great, just the way I planned.

Along the way Patty and I began to struggle with spiritual issues; we realized there was a void in our life. Somehow, all of our worldly successes and possessions were not fulfilling our needs. Patty began to search for answers. Her sister had been sending her tracts that spoke of man's sinfulness and need of a Savior. Shortly after reading those tracts, Patty accepted Jesus Christ as her personal Savior. She now wanted to attend church, and a friend at work recommended one. We began to attend and received several visits from the pastor. At this point I was only mildly interested and admitted I was unsure about my spiritual condition. As the weeks went on the pastor helped me see that one is permitted into heaven by faith in Jesus Christ, not by merely living a good life.

Several months later I desired eternal life and realized my need of a Savior. I accepted God's free gift of eternal life through the work of Jesus Christ and trusted in Jesus' death and sacrifice for the forgiveness of my sin. Patty and I became active in a local church. I held church offices, taught Sunday school, and enjoyed the fellowship. I was still living out my dream. I had specific plans for my family and for my children's lives. Somehow, God's plan and mine seemed to be in harmony.

I still felt in control. Life was going the way I had planned, but then the dreams began to unravel. Things began to happen that were not part of my plan. My career began to flutter and my marriage began to lose its brilliance. I had reached forty years of age and seemed to be experiencing a midlife crisis. I realized later I had not truly yielded control of my life to Jesus Christ even though I was trusting in Him alone for salvation.

The death of my son was the final blow. This single event destroyed all remaining sense of being in control. I could not protect my son even when he lay in his own bed.

Patty and I always tried to protect our children; we did not let them do anything risky or dangerous. Several months before Kelly died, he asked repeatedly if he could have a dirt bike. We naturally told him no because they were so dangerous.

When I think about protecting my children, where is one of the safest places for them? At home in bed. Yet that is where my son died. There are no safe places, nowhere death's arms cannot reach.

Therefore, I concluded I really did not have control over anything in my life. So, here I was, a control person who had realized he was out of control. This was a very insecure position. After running through all the logical alternatives, I knew there was only one way that leads to peace. I must trust in a Holy God. I must have faith and believe His plan is being played out in me. If *I* am not in control, I must believe *He* is. Therein lies the means of having the "peace that passes all understanding." When all things are crashing in around me and I have the feeling of being totally out of control, can I still have peace? No matter what happens, can I put my trust in the fact that God is working out His perfect plan?

After Kelly died, I realized that I had never truly given my children up to God. I had been holding on to them, wanting them to be what I wanted. As I think back, I can even recall not wanting my boys to be pastors because a pastor's life is so hard. I wanted them to have an easier life. I acknowledged my children did not belong to me and God was more than able to come and get them anytime He pleased, regardless of how tightly I might hold on to them. I am in no way suggesting this is why Kelly died. God did not take my child because I had failed to give him over to the Lord. I did not have control over my children any more than I had control over anything else in life. As I held onto them ever so tightly, I had created a false assurance of keeping them within the safety of our family and home.

After reaching this conclusion, I totally gave my children up to God. I said, "They are Yours, Lord, to do with as You please. Use them for Your service and glory." I knew whatever God chose to do with them, even if it included trial and tribulation, it was okay. His plan was perfect, even if it did not appear as such from a human perspective.

The Guilt

Guilt is always present in the grief process because there are words left unsaid, actions left undone, dreams unfulfilled, and thoughts never followed through. Guilt is magnified in the aftermath of a child's death. Patty and I were told that 80 percent of the marriages that experience the death of a child end in divorce, and I believe guilt is a major contributor to that statistic. Our nature seeks to blame someone every time something goes wrong. In grief one usually seeks to blame self or shift that blame to another. This blame shifting is a common tool used in an attempt to remove guilt and can be devastating in a marriage relationship. Blaming self frequently results in withdrawal and separation. Blaming others creates dissension and confrontation. Both of these actions are detrimental to a marriage and can be overwhelming when added on top of normal grief.

For me guilt took on unique aspects that I had to deal with. Children are a parent's responsibility; we have an inherent calling to protect and nurture them. I have become convinced a parent must contend with guilt when a child dies, regardless of the circumstances. One must deal with feelings of failure. How could I have been so insensitive to let my son die quietly in his bed without even the slightest recognition something abnormal was happening? There were warning signs as I think back. Why didn't I recognize them and react? The doctors reassured us nothing could have been done, even if I had known Kelly was having a cerebral hemorrhage. But their reassurance did not eliminate my guilt and my feeling that I should have done something.

I felt guilty for the last discipline I applied. I recalled the last time I yelled at Kelly. He and one of his friends were throwing the soccer ball up on the garage roof and it got stuck. As I came outside I saw them attempting to dislodge the ball with a long stick. My patience was short that day and I began to yell at him. I now felt so guilty about the interaction. What was the big deal about the ball being caught on the roof? Why didn't I just wrap him up in my arms and tell him it was okay? Why didn't I just hug him instead of yelling at him?

The Alien Syndrome

Several days after the funeral I was faced with the question of when I should return to normal activities. And when should I go back to work? One can only remain curled up in the fetal position for a little while.

I stayed home for one week after Kelly's funeral before realizing that staying at home was not making me feel any better. So I gathered myself together and headed back into the workplace.

I recall the first time I entered the cafeteria at work, a large room that seats several hundred people. It was as if everyone in the room was looking at me and saying to themselves, "There is the man whose son died." The people were not really staring at me, but that was how it felt.

Grief made me very self-conscious around others. At work and elsewhere, it became very difficult for me to enter into normal conversation, because I would immediately realize my value system had changed and was nowhere close to anybody else's. I felt as if no one understood me, no one was able to relate to me, no one was like me, and no one could feel my pain. I felt I was all alone; I was an alien.

Is my thinking distorted? I asked myself. *Is my view of life so drastically different from everyone else's?* I was a

45

different person, and my view of this world *was* very different. I had been to a place most people do not go. I had walked a path most people never trod. I felt as if I was living in a foreign country and did not speak the language. I felt isolated and removed from normality. I wondered if I would ever return to normal. Was there any way of going back to the way things used to be? I concluded my past life was over and I had entered into a new world. Emotionally and spiritually I had metamorphosed. Relationships were not the same: Some of my old friends seemed as strangers, and I no longer related to others as I had before.

Changes in life are normal. We all change as we mature. Friends come and go. However, most of these changes happen very slowly and occur over years. My son's death had catapulted me into a new environment in which I had no preparation for living. It was as if I had dropped by parachute into a foreign country and was now expected to live a normal life like everyone else; I was not prepared for the change. All I wanted to do was go back where I came from, back where things were safe and secure. But, the reality was, there was no return. There was no going back.

Life Goes On

It is amazing how activity goes on around you as your life seems to stop. Even as you drag your feet, life pulls you along. Life is like a locomotive going down the track. Very few things can stop it.

Kelly died in February, and I can recall sitting down to do the income tax the following month. I remember thinking, *I should be released from this responsibility. I should be granted a reprieve. Doesn't the IRS understand my son has died? Wouldn't it be okay to just forget the taxes for this year?* There are no excuses; life goes on!

I had to continue working. I had to go to the grocery store, buy food, and continue eating. I had to fix the car when it broke down. I had to cut the grass. Life goes on! Isn't it amazing—if my heart keeps beating, I must do these mundane things that seem so unimportant.

This fact became even more irritating as I observed those around me. Did my son's death impact their lives or did they forget it moments after his funeral and move on to the next event? I must admit I frequently became angry. It seemed as if others quickly returned to "normal" while I was forced to deal with my grief day after day after day.

The Grace Period

People are very gracious for the first couple of months; they are mindful of your tragedy and think they understand what you are going through. After all, everyone has had a similar experience. Their ninety-year-old grandmother may have died; they may have suffered through the death of a pet during childhood. Therefore, they understand. But the death of a child, your child, is worlds apart from any of those experiences. Those other experiences do not even remotely come close!

Some people are wise enough to admit they have no idea what you are going through. Some are sensitive enough to tell you they cannot even begin to understand the pain. Most people, though, have not experienced real grief and find it almost impossible to understand your feelings. They want you to get better and get on with life for their sake. Your grief makes them uncomfortable. While a few compassionate people are willing to give you all the time you need, most have expectations of your getting on with life after a couple of months. They are unaware how long the road is. The death of a child becomes a lifelong journey with many crooked bends.

Two years after Kelly's death I was asked to participate on a panel for a church seminar on parenting. During the panel I spoke of his death and recounted the impact it had on my approach to Shane and Bethany. A man who had also lost a son came up to me after the panel and asked me how long my son had been dead. I told him two years. His response was, "Oh, you are so new." It had been seven years for him. I am sure he was reflecting back on how fresh his pain was at the two-year mark.

I have talked to couples whose child has been dead for ten years. The pain and difficulty are still there. The pointedness of the pain is less but still present. Tears still well up as they recount the death of their child.

It then becomes inexcusable to me when people are so bold to say, "It is time to get on with your life." Yet these are the very words I have heard spoken by insensitive people who have no personal experience with death. No person has the right to tell another when to stop grieving or move on. God, in His infinite grace, works it out with each one on an individual basis.

I have two pictures of Kelly on my desk at work. One of them is a picture of him in his seventh-grade basketball uniform. One day a manager at work stopped by to chit-chat. He remarked about my little basketball player. I informed him my son had died two years before. He reeled back and expressed his condolence. I told him of my hope of seeing my son again one day when I joined him in heaven. His parting words were, "I am glad to see that you have it behind you." I said nothing as I bit my lip and excused him in my mind as another person who had no comprehension of the extent of grief. At that moment I hoped I would never get Kelly's death "behind me."

Oh, dear Lord, I miss my little boy.

I miss his smiling face and his deep dimples.

I miss the warmth of his affection, his hugs, and kisses.

I miss his voice and his "I love you, Dad."

I miss his laughter and his joy for living.

I miss the noise of his friends.

I miss seeing him curled up on the couch with his afghan watching TV.

I miss him sitting on his bed doing his homework.

I miss his "boom box" and the songs he played.

I miss his white hair and his blue eyes.

I miss watching him play basketball and soccer.

I miss him so much!

May 31

Chapter 3

Hitting Bottom

The Deep Pit of Despair

The deepest of despair was not in the days immediately after Kelly died, but months down the road. My mind was a blur for the first few months. I was numb and capable of dealing with only a few basic issues. It was months later when the reality of my son's death began to take hold. I began to realize the heartache was not going away and I was going to be forced to live with it for my remaining life. Could I endure the pain for a lifetime? The darkness became oppressive.

My first forty years of life had been so easy. I had never been able to understand anyone who was experiencing depression. I could not fathom why someone would commit suicide. My solution to life's problems was always so simple: Think about positive things and things will get better. That solution did not even begin to touch my feelings. I was now face-to-face with one of life's greatest struggles, maybe the most difficult. I cried every morning in the

51

shower, all the way to work, and all the way home at night. Sometimes during the day at work I was overwhelmed with grief and had to close my office door. This continued for six months. As I experienced the refining fire, the Lord was purging me of all sense of self-sufficiency. I got to the point where I could not even get out of bed in the morning without asking for the Lord's help. There was no longer anything I could do within my own strength. So, there I was, a virtual ball of mass with no form and no purpose. My dreams had been shattered. I was at the bottom of the pit.

I began to relate to King David as he lamented: "My wounds fester and are loathsome because of my sinful folly. I am bowed down and brought very low; all day long I go about mourning. My back is filled with searing pain; there is no health in my body. I am feeble and utterly crushed; I groan in anguish of heart" (Ps. 38:5–8).

I was also at the crossroads of faith: *Do I embrace all my spiritual training or do I cast God aside? Do I turn from Him in bitterness or draw close to Him for comfort? Do I believe the promises of God or reject them?* If I rejected God's promises, then my hope of ever seeing Kelly again was dead. My hope of eternal life would be crushed.

At this point it became a battle of the wills. Satan sought to destroy me and my faith while God held onto my very soul. I had been a Christian for fifteen years. I had enough spiritual knowledge to last a lifetime. I had been rooted in God's Word, and I knew His promises. It was application time. The rubber had finally met the road in my spiritual life.

Recognizing all my unanswered questions, I wondered whether I could hold onto God's promises. I was at the same point as Peter when Jesus prayed for him: "Simon, Simon, Satan has asked to sift you as wheat. But I have prayed for you, Simon, that your faith may not fail" (Luke 22:31–32).

My faith was experiencing the ultimate test. Satan whispered, "There is no life after death. This earth is all there is." I did not have the strength within myself to beat Satan at his own game. Doubt and despair became the devil's jaws as he sought to devour me. Just as the apostle Peter said, "Your enemy the devil prowls around like a roaring lion looking for someone to devour" (1 Peter 5:8).

The bottom line was, "Do I believe the Bible is God's Word and is it His truth? Are the promises with which I am so familiar true?"

The Spiritual Battle

Over and over I would order things in my mind, remembering God's promises and recalling my scriptural knowledge concerning eternal life:

Heaven is better than this earth.
We are to look forward to heaven.
God wants us to be with Him.
My son is happier being in heaven than he was being on
    this earth.

And so the arguments went. I would seek to convince myself it was better Kelly had died. I tried to find some positive feeling to offset the overwhelming agony. I tried to tell myself it was okay.

One can spend hours getting the logic in order, getting the arguments in line, and preparing the case. But, in a matter of milliseconds all the arguments, all the neatly ordered logic falls apart. The reality rolls in like the evening tide, washing away all those hours of thought, every one of those foolish arguments, all that reasoning. The agony again sets in. The reality of life rears its ugly head. I miss my child. I cannot talk to him, I cannot see him, I cannot touch him, I cannot smell him, I cannot hear his laughter, I cannot yell at him. He is gone! His spirit evaporated to a different world.

Was my faith weak? Was I a disgrace to my church? Was I failing to trust God? I answered those questions loudly, "No!" This was the conflict between my spiritual being and my earthly being. I knew God's promises, but I was still a father who missed his son. The pain of separation was real, and it coexisted with my spiritual understanding.

Again and again, I repeated this process. As if climbing a mountain, I would get my spiritual reasoning in order and tell myself I felt better. Then all the arguments would fall apart and I would tumble back down into the valley. Up and down, day after day, this was the cycle of grief.

Confrontations

As a result of Kelly's death I had a keener sense of discernment. My eyes were more fully open to the existence of the spiritual world. I knew Satan was real, not just a fantasy character. Within a year of Kelly's death I had two experiences that were quite possibly spiritual encounters.

One was the first Father's Day after Kelly died. I decided that I was not able to go to church and would go instead to Paul's Place, a friend's wooded lot in a secluded area not far from our home. Shane, Kelly, and I had cut firewood there many times; it was a very special place to our family. A creek winds its way along the property, and it was always a peaceful place to visit. So I decided to go there alone while the rest of the family went to church. I took some of my writings for meditation. Upon arrival at Paul's Place I parked the car and made my way down the hill to the creek. There was a place in the creek where it made a bend. Along the bank were large boulders on which we had sat many times to rest and listen to the babbling water. I sat and read my writings.

After meditating, I decided I would take a walk up the creek. I laid my writings on one of the gray boulders and made my way into the cold water leaving my shoes on to protect my feet from the rocks. It was a warm day, and the sun was shining through the branches of the large trees. I walked up the creek farther than I had ever been before. I was secluded, totally by myself. The only sight or sound of life was an occasional bird. As I turned around and headed back I was immersed in thoughts of Kelly. I wanted to communicate with him. I had left my writings on the rock and I thought, *If only an angel would pick them up and take them to Kelly.* I told myself if they were not on the rock when I returned, an angel would have taken them.

Suddenly, I was startled by a grotesque scream, like nothing I had ever heard. I felt the ground shake, and it sounded as if a huge animal like an elephant was running through the woods. I froze in my steps as shivers went down my back. My mind sought to match up the sound with some prior bit of stored information. My mind drew a blank, no match. What was it? The only remote match was that it might be a large buck. But the scream was too human-like, and no buck could be large enough to shake the ground and make the sounds I heard. I slowly moved toward the bank of the creek and peered into the woods. I saw nothing. I stood still and listened intently for any other sounds, still nothing. What had it been? Was it possible that I had heard a spirit world confrontation between a demon and an angel? Was the demon stalking me and taken by surprise by the attack of the angel? I did not write this off as a foolish idea.

After remaining at the edge of the creek for several minutes, afraid to move or breathe, I proceeded cautiously down the creek to my starting point. To my disappointment, my writings remained lying on the large rock where I had left them.

My second encounter was one night in a deep sleep. My memory is vivid for a few brief seconds. I remember being confronted by a demon face-to-face. I looked the demon straight in the eye and said, "I'm not afraid of you." In an immediate response I was sucked out of my bed, taken through the wall, and carried down the street at a tremendous rate of speed, eight to ten feet off the surface of the road. It was like riding in a jet fighter, but I was freely suspended in the air. It was over as fast as it happened, and I was returned to my bed. Was the demon's action in response to my boldness? Was it just a dream or something more?

I have contemplated these two occurrences often, considering them in the light of other accounts I have heard. Why is it some people have these encounters while others do not? Why is it that often great periods of time elapse between such encounters? Why is it sometimes these experiences run together and occur in groups? I have developed a theory to answer these questions and have tested it against my own experiences.

Is it possible, during periods of great tribulation or spiritual struggle when we are broken even to the point of being forsaken of life, we become the greatest threat to Satan? I believe it is. In such a state, we have lost all fear of death and would willingly die or sacrifice our life; Satan would have no power over us. There would be no fear he could use to manipulate our minds. In such a state, God has full control to do with us as He pleases. I can see how fearful Satan would be.

Is it possible in these instances Satan draws even closer to us, so close we are at the very edge of the spiritual world, so close we even scuff the edge and can see a dim view or a glimpse of the spiritual world? I believe this is so.

The apostle Paul spoke of such encounters in Ephesians 6:12: "For our struggle is not against flesh and blood, but against the rulers, against the authorities, against the powers of this dark world and against the spiritual forces of evil in the heavenly realms."

Why is it that we so easily dismiss the supernatural? Why is it that we shy away from it or write it off? Could it be Satan does not desire us to take such events seriously?

Oh, dear Lord, how I long to be with You,

To taste the sweetness of heaven,

To see the beauties that I cannot imagine,

To know the peace flowing from Your infinite wisdom,

To feel the warmth of Your everlasting love,

To see my Kelly,

To be reunited again with wholeness of family,

To relax and know that never again shall we be separated.

May 16

Chapter 4

Hope Returns

Confrontation with the Enemy

At the bottom of the pit I was faced with three questions. Do I wither and die or struggle to climb out? Do I confront the enemy or succumb to the onslaught? Do I believe in God's Word or reject it?

The bottom of the pit is a lonely place where one despairs of life itself. It is a place where one can easily succumb to the weight of the burden by just rolling over and giving up. It is a place where Satan seeks to keep you as he encourages you to give up the fight. In this dark place Satan tells you God's promises are not true and hope is a wasted thought.

I am convinced that I did not make the decision on my own to begin the climb out of the pit. God drew me unto Himself. I realized I had met my match with Satan, and, if I tried to conquer the enemy by myself, I would not succeed.

In desperation I reached out to Jesus. I was now prepared to give up everything. Every part of my being that had not been given to Jesus Christ was now His. I succumbed to God's right to do with my family and me as He pleased. I was a broken man. My agenda had been destroyed, and I was now ready to follow His agenda. Life was not going to fulfill my dreams; I would have to submit to His order and pre-determined events.

God purges us for His purposes. Oswald Chambers describes this purging when he says, "Complete weakness and dependence will always be the occasion for the Spirit of God to manifest His power."[1] Once I was drained of all sense of self-sufficiency, humbled at the Lord's feet, and yielded to Him, the Spirit was free to move within me. I was in the process of being equipped to be used of God.

The return journey had begun, but the climb was to be steep and long.

A Turning Point

In the midst of severe grief, I often felt life was hopeless. I had little desire to live and even had thoughts of asking God to put me out of my agony. Somewhere along the way, I experienced a turning point; however, it was so gradual I could not tell you when it occurred. It is imperative to realize that, even after the turning point, life was not grand. In my opinion, moments and significant periods of depression are part and parcel with grief. Grievers should not be afraid or embarrassed to seek counsel though, if the depression becomes overwhelming.

Even with returning hope, life for the griever is up and down. Although the distance between the peaks and valley grows wider with time, I do not expect to complete the journey in this life.

God's Mercy

God promises to deliver those who cry out to Him. "The righteous cry out, and the LORD hears them; he delivers them from all their troubles. The LORD is close to the brokenhearted and saves those who are crushed in spirit. A righteous man may have many troubles, but the LORD delivers him from them all; he protects all his bones, not one of them will be broken" (Ps. 34:17–20). Even though God permits and even creates adversity, He is readily able and willing to respond to our cry for help. God may even hide Himself from us during the adversity; however, He promises to reappear and reveal Himself after a while. "O people of Zion, who live in Jerusalem, you will weep no more. How gracious he will be when you cry for help! As soon as he hears, he will answer you. Although the Lord gives you the bread of adversity and the water of affliction, your teachers will be hidden no more; with your own eyes you will see them" (Isa. 30:19–20).

Isaiah reaffirms two truths. One, God may give me adversity and affliction, and two, He will respond to my cry for help at the time of His choosing.

Grief can be overwhelming at times, but God is merciful in that He lets us deal with little pieces of grief rather than forcing us to deal with it all at once. God is like the mother feeding the infant. The wise mother feeds the infant a little at a time permitting proper digestion of the milk. If fed too quickly, the baby cannot cope with the volume and vomits it back into the mother's lap. I am convinced if I had to deal with the totality of my son's death all at once it would be too crushing for me to bear.

61

So, in His mercy, God grants brief reprieves from the agony. He gives us moments of rest from the work of grieving.

Good Dreams

Frequently, people share dreams in which a loved one who has died is speaking to them from heaven and reassuring the dreamer they are okay. Anyone who has experienced the death of a loved one wants that reassurance, and it is as if the dream provides what the soul desires.

Patty was the first one to have a dream about Kelly. When she told me about it, I was envious of her, and I longed to have a dream too. Mine did not come for several months; then one night, for no apparent reason, I had my first dream. It was wonderful to again interact with Kelly. In the dream I could talk to him, touch him, and hold him. A dream is like an interactive video, which is much more meaningful than still pictures.

One of my dreams I remember very well. In it Kelly came back to life. You cannot even begin to comprehend the elation I felt. I remember how excited I was about taking him to church. I wanted everyone to see Kelly was again alive and with me.

All my dreams of Kelly have been about light-hearted frolics that took place in this life. I have had no dreams where he communicates to me from heaven. I am thankful I have not had any nightmares about Kelly's death. While it invades my conscious thoughts, I have not had to relive it in dreams.

In each dream Kelly is younger than he was when he died. When he died he was twelve years old, and his age seems to be eight or ten in each of my dreams. I cannot explain this. These dreams have not occurred very often. I only have them two or three times a year, but I cherish each one and long for the next.

My experience with dreams reaffirms the uniqueness of grief for each individual. My dreams will not be like someone else's dreams. My response to grief will not be the same as another person's. Each person is unique, and each experience will be different.

My Friend

In the days and months after Kelly died I sought out a friend—someone who could understand my feelings, someone who would listen to my thoughts. As I reached out to people through letters and conversations, I found no one who felt what I felt, no one who understood what I was going through. I was like a radio telescope that sends radio waves into space, seeking to connect with some other being in the universe. Time after time I would send out my radio waves and receive no response.

For that whole first year I looked for a friend who understood. On my birthday, one year and one month after my son's death, a friend gave me a copy of *My Utmost for His Highest* by Oswald Chambers, an English pastor in the early 1900s. As I read this daily devotional prepared from his sermons and Bible studies, I realized I had finally found someone who felt what I felt. I had finally found the long-sought-after friend who knew what I was going through. He could not listen to me, but I could listen to him.

Time and time again, God used these writings to console me, to give me insight into His Word, and to teach me new lessons. It was through Oswald Chambers's writings that God introduced me to the reality of suffering, the need to accept it, and to see it as a tool in His hand.

The Hope

Where there is pain and suffering, hope is offered. "Therefore, we do not lose heart. Though outwardly we are wasting away, yet inwardly we are being renewed day by day. For our light and momentary troubles are achieving for us an eternal glory that far outweighs them all. So we fix our eyes not on what is seen, but on what is unseen. For what is seen is temporary, but what is unseen is eternal" (2 Cor. 4:16–18).

The apostle Paul offers encouragement when he says, "do not lose heart." He admits we are wasting away, yet the troubles of this life are creating a spiritual renewal within us. This transformation is the conforming work of God as He molds us in the image of Christ. God uses the difficulties of life to change our hearts and to create in us a new perspective on life. There are unlimited trials and tribulations we must endure, but there is hope for those who rest in the promises of God. This hope is based on an eternal reward that makes pale the trials of this life.

Paul encourages us to view the troubles as only "light and momentary," for one day they will seem insignificant in comparison to the reward of eternal life. The fruit of our labor will not be in vain. We are to "fix our eyes" on the eternal life that cannot be seen. Paul tells us the things that are seen, the things of this world, are temporary. It is that which we cannot see, namely eternal life, which is everlasting.

During the early months of grieving a friend gave me a tape on which was a song by Wayne Watson. The song speaks of the trial and tribulation of death and the eventual and ultimate healing some will experience if they trust in Jesus Christ. Watson suggests we will be "home free" when we experience the "ultimate healing."

Out in the corridor we pray for life
A mother for her baby
A husband for his wife
Sometimes the good die young
It's sad but true
And while we pray for one more heartbeat
The real comfort is with You.

Home free—eventually
At the ultimate healing
We will be home free
Home free
Oh, I've got a feeling
At the ultimate healing
We will be home free.[2]

No matter how severe my grief, no matter how deep my pain, I shall one day experience the "ultimate healing" when I stand before God and enter eternal life. This too is the hope to which I hold.

Time and time again I have felt like a prisoner, caught within my misery, never to be released. But God does promise deliverance from the oppression of life. Isaiah spoke as the forerunner of Christ when he said, "He has sent me to bind up the brokenhearted, to proclaim freedom for the captives and release for the prisoners" (Isa. 61:1).

I give testimony that Jesus Christ brings healing and can "bind up the brokenhearted." I do not feel completely released from prison, but I have been delivered from solitary confinement into a less dark cell. I am looking forward to the day of complete release when I am delivered from this body and God grants me the new body shaped for eternity. This shall be the moment of complete healing and total deliverance. There shall be eternal freedom from all disasters, all illness, and all calamity. The shackles of this life shall be unlocked and thrown away.

Hope is offered to everyone. Some choose to accept it while others reject it. God offers us the promise of eternity. Do we embrace it or turn away?

I am reminded of Hebrews 11:1: "Now faith is being sure of what we hope for and certain of what we do not see." Hope and faith are tied together. One rests in the other. I hope there is a heaven beyond this life; I hope to see my son again in heaven. Faith is when I believe in this hope with certainty. Faith is being sure heaven exists and trusting in Jesus Christ to deliver me through His sacrifice or atonement for my sins. I cannot see heaven. I have no worldly proof it exists. There is no scientific logic to support it. Yet, God has instilled within me the faith to believe in it.

The pain is real, and I am not to pretend it is not there. However, by God's grace I can extract myself from the muck and mire of suffering and focus on my heavenly reward. I must choose to not dwell on the things of this world, those things that are seen. I must concentrate on the spiritual life awaiting those who trust in Christ. I must have hope in the eternal life that I cannot see and have no proof exists. This is faith. This is hope.

Isaiah recorded God's promise of a coming time when we shall enter the City of Zion, God's dwelling place. This too is the focus of my hope.

> And a highway will be there;
>   it will be called the Way of Holiness.
> The unclean will not journey on it;
>   it will be for those who walk in that Way;
>   wicked fools will not go about on it.
> No lion will be there,
>   nor will any ferocious beast get up on it;
>   they will not be found there.
> But only the redeemed will walk there,
>   and the ransomed of the LORD will return.

> They will enter Zion with singing;
>> everlasting joy will crown their heads.
> Gladness and joy will overtake them,
>> and sorrow and sighing will flee away.
>
> Isaiah 35:8–10

The highway or the "Way of Holiness" is the pathway to heaven. A pathway reserved for God's people. Those who trust in Jesus Christ, "the redeemed," shall enter Zion, or heaven, and everlasting joy shall be their crown.

Likewise, Isaiah describes God's protection of His people, those He has called as His own. God is promising to see us through whatever tribulation we face. No matter what the trial, He shall usher us through, hand in hand as we go.

> "Fear not, for I have redeemed you;
>> I have called you by name; you are mine.
> When you pass through the waters,
>> I will be with you;
> and when you pass through the rivers,
>> they will not sweep over you.
> When you walk through the fire,
>> you will not be burned;
>> the flames will not set you ablaze.
> For I am the LORD, your God,
>> the Holy One of Israel, your Savior."
>
> Isaiah 43:1–3

The prophet Habakkuk offers another perspective as the Babylonians, a brutal and arrogant lot, are invading Judah.

> Yet I will wait patiently for the day of calamity
>> to come on the nation invading us.
> Though the fig tree does not bud
>> and there are no grapes on the vine,
> though the olive crop fails
>> and the fields produce no food,

though there are no sheep in the pen
and no cattle in the stalls,
yet I will rejoice in the LORD,
I will be joyful in God my Savior.
Habakkuk 3:16–18

Considering this passage, Henry Halley said, "Faith is the ability to feel so sure of God, that, no matter how dark the day, there is no doubt as to the outcome. For God's people there is a glorious future. It may be a long way off. But it is absolutely sure."[3]

Faith is the only basis for true hope.

Paul's Encouragement

The apostle Paul offered great insight and encouragement in his letter to the Thessalonians. The Thessalonians had experienced the kinship of suffering and had demonstrated great faith even in the midst of tribulation. "You became imitators of us and of the Lord; in spite of severe suffering" (1 Thess. 1:6a).

In addition to their own sufferings, the Thessalonians were likewise upset by what Paul and Timothy were being forced to endure. Paul said they should not be unsettled by these happenings but understand that God has ordained all their circumstances: "We sent Timothy, who is our brother and God's fellow worker in spreading the gospel of Christ, to strengthen and encourage you in your faith, so that no one would be unsettled by these trials. You know quite well that we were destined for them" (1 Thess. 3:2–3).

Are Christians today an exception to Christians of the Bible or are we, likewise, destined to suffer?

After acknowledging the commonplace occurrence and acceptance of trials, Paul goes on to offer encouragement and suggest a response: "Be joyful always; pray continually; give thanks in all circumstances, for this is God's will for you in Christ Jesus" (1 Thess. 5:16–18).

Paul suggests in the midst of trials we are to:

1. Be joyful—look beyond the current suffering and rest in the promise of God's ultimate deliverance.
2. Pray continually—trust in Him to see us through the pain of the moment and ask Him to give us strength to endure the next few minutes.
3. Give thanks—be grateful for what God will do through you as a result of the experience; give thanks for the fruit God will produce in you.

These are positive steps we can take to rise above the tribulation. Although Paul could not remove the trials the Thessalonians were experiencing, he could offer relief from the pain and provide a perspective that would help them endure the suffering. This same action is applicable to today's trials.

Paul's Perseverance

During Paul's missionary trip to Iconium as described in Acts 14, Paul preached the gospel and performed many miracles, stirring up much dissension. We read in verse 5: "There was a plot afoot among the Gentiles and Jews, together with their leaders, to mistreat them and stone them."

Paul then proceeded to Lystra, Derbe, and the surrounding country. Again he generated much excitement by his healing ministry. However, the Jews from Antioch and Iconium followed as we read in verse 19: "Then some Jews came from Antioch and Iconium and won the crowd over. They stoned Paul and dragged him outside the city, thinking he was dead."

Paul was stoned and left for dead, but by God's grace he was revived and went on to Derbe to continue preaching. We read, "They preached the good news in that city and won a large number of disciples. Then they returned to Lystra, Iconium and Antioch, strengthening the disciples and encouraging them to remain true to the faith. 'We must go through many hardships to enter the kingdom of God,' they said" (Acts 14:21–22).

It is amazing Paul returned to the very people who had stoned him and left him for dead. What an encouragement and example of perseverance. Even under the threat of death, Paul returned to the believers in Antioch and Iconium to encourage them in the faith. His mission would not be deterred by fear of man or any other calamity.

Paul concludes with the reminder, "we must go through many hardships." Again there is this reminder, life is not easy nor has it been planned to be such and there is no permission granted to be distraught or pitied because of tribulation or trial. There is an admission that hardship is part of the process designed by God, and as a result, our hope is not to be dampened or destroyed.

Paul further suggests that hope is the product of suffering: "Not only so, but we also rejoice in our sufferings, because we know that suffering produces perseverance; perseverance, character; and character, hope. And hope does not disappoint us, because God has poured out his love into our hearts by the Holy Spirit, whom he has given us" (Rom. 5:3–5).

Suffering produces perseverance, character, and hope. To the best of my knowledge, no other means creates these worthy attributes.

Dear Lord, there is so much that we do not understand or comprehend about life. Our minds are finite, yet our proud nature wants to think that we know so much. And on occasion, You select those to humble. Oh, how You can jerk us into place and remind us of our lowly position before Your mighty throne. Oh, how powerful and great is Your fatherly hand.

I am humbled before You, dear Lord, cast to my knees. Thankful that You are a loving God who cares for me and my family. A God who is in control of each moment, and a God who has already laid out a lifelong plan that You are executing with a most gentle touch.

July 11

Chapter 5

Seeking Understanding

The Search

I went through a period where I wanted to understand everything. Why did my son die? Why was I feeling what I was feeling? Were my feelings okay? I began to read and search for answers. My primary target was the Bible. What did God's Word say about suffering and tribulation? In addition, I read numerous books on the subject of grief.

This chapter attempts to identify the issues I dealt with and the conclusions I reached. I suggest that my issues are very similar to the issues most would have to deal with who are experiencing suffering and tribulation. My conclusions may not be the same as others; however, I attempt to describe my logic and provide supporting commentary.

The Suffering

Suffering is unpleasant. We try to avoid it. We pray, asking God to spare us from all suffering, whether it be sickness, grief, financial difficulty, or otherwise. If we do accept that God uses suffering, we attribute it mostly to His discipline, again a negative experience. Suffering is clouded by prosperity theology, which claims God only wishes happiness and good health for His people, those who have enough faith. Little is said about suffering as a positive experience. Most would not see it as something that is good for us.

So, is suffering a product of sin? Should we blame Satan for suffering or recognize it as originating from a Holy God? If we can't understand it and it hurts, it must be bad. If it is bad, it must come from Satan. So the logic continues, reinforcing that suffering is something to be avoided, something that only befalls the wicked or those of little faith.

Our Lord Jesus was a man of suffering. He knew it well. He knew His ultimate mission was draped in suffering, and He experienced it all the way to Calvary. Isaiah 53:3 says, "He was . . . a man of sorrows, and familiar with suffering."

Christ also knew that the Christian life was to be adorned with suffering. In John 16:33, He said, "In this world you will have trouble. But take heart! I have overcome the world." Note the affirmative "will." Not "maybe." If you are a believer in Christ "you *will* have trouble." This is stated as a fact. There are no options. If life has been grand up to now for you, thank God for His mercy and enjoy the moment. If you have undergone tribulation, do not feel alone. You are in the company of God's people.

Jesus offers encouragement to those of us who must walk the road of suffering and urges us to take the eternal perspective, to look through the tunnel at the fruitful land on the other side. Scripture reminds us this life is but a passing moment. Can we endure a pain that is only momentary? There is an eternal relief, a healing, for those who willingly wait and trust in God's promise of an eternal life, a place of peace and comfort.

The apostle Peter, after much suffering, captured the same perspective as Christ when he said, "Dear friends, do not be surprised at the painful trial you are suffering, as though something strange were happening to you. But rejoice that you participate in the sufferings of Christ, so that you may be overjoyed when his glory is revealed" (1 Peter 4:12–13). One would assume, if we are not to be surprised at suffering, it is a common occurrence. Yet often we who suffer ask God that painful question, "Why me, Lord; why has this not befallen my brother or sister?" Peter does not let well enough alone. After telling us not to be surprised, he goes on to say we are to rejoice, not in our agony but in what accompanies it. Peter suggests there are benefits to suffering and we should strive to see through the moment. Is it possible there might be some good in the awful experience? Peter contends it unites us with Christ. It further extends the fellowship. Suffering makes our bond with Jesus grow stronger. It heightens our passion for Him and causes the flame of love to burn hotter.

Have you ever endured a painful trial or hard times with someone else? Kelly's death was the most difficult trial Patty and I have had to endure. I cannot imagine anything in this life that could ever be as difficult as experiencing the death of your child. This single event not only changed us individually, but it completely reworked our marriage. My relationship with Patty was solidified in a supernatural way. We now had a oneness of mind and heart that had not existed before. I believe our relationship is now on an unshakable foundation. The summer after Kelly died I wrote the following letter to Patty:

My dearest Patricia,

I write this that I might eternally record my deepest feelings for you. I love you for choosing to share our lives together, the ups and downs, the joys and sorrows, the laughter and the tears, the hard labor and sweat, and the intimate moments of closeness. We have shared the carefree joys of youth and the maturing experiences that come with growing together. We were together to experience the elation of childbirth and the deepest sadness of losing our Kelly. We have felt the insecurity of a faltering marriage and the renewal of recommital. We have fought and clashed our wills and humbled ourselves to the needs of each other. We have labored together to raise our children and instill God honoring values. You have been a most worthy partner, caring mother, and true friend. I wish we could have been spared the sadness of life, however, we have learned to appreciate the blessings, realized that life is not fair, and found that the only comfort lies in trusting God's promises. We have risen out of the quagmire of earth's entrapments and are able to look forward to life's rewards after death, while having a new understanding and appreciation for this life.

We have experienced life's greatest tragedy and have not lost our hope, in fact, our hope has been steadfast and strengthened. You are to be admired for your combined strength and sensitivity. God has blessed us by letting us participate in the creation and nurturing of three lovely children who have high ideals and an understanding of the correct priorities of life.

Together, may we live out this life and look forward to spending eternity with our Lord and Savior.

I love you, Jehu

In this modern world, we encourage training functions where people work through some difficult task together for the purpose of building teamwork and stronger relationships. In our weakness we do acknowledge the benefits of tough experiences, but we can only see that to a point. God extends the concept way beyond our fleshly thresholds. God uses the kinship of suffering to solidify and develop our relationship with Christ. Through our suffering we are able to empathize with the suffering our Lord Jesus endured, and the Holy Spirit uses the pain to build a stronger bond of love with Jesus Christ. Likewise, Peter further suggests there is a product, a joy, when Christ's glory is revealed. Is it possible we would appreciate Christ less if we did not experience suffering? I can confirm there is a longing for Christ that exists only in those who have suffered—a desire to see Him; a desire to be removed from the agony of this life; a desire to be united with Christ and to have the eternal peace. Someone wrote a poem that ends, "We would not long for heaven if earth held only joy."

So, we are driven back to the question, "Does God use suffering for His purposes?" Oswald Chambers had keen insight into this when he said, "What a revelation it is to know that sorrow and bereavement and suffering are the clouds that come along with God. God cannot come near without clouds. He does not come in clear shining."[1]

I have become convinced that Scripture and Chambers's comments do not conflict. My condensed version of his statement would read, "We do not learn anything on a sunny day." As I reflect back, I conclude we do not learn anything on a sunny day because we are too engrossed in enjoying the moment. Prosperity and good times only contribute to our attachment to this world. They do not instill any desire for the eternal world. I cannot recall one time in my life when good times drove me to my knees, seeking the mercy of a Holy God! I am not saying I should not be thankful for happy events in my life. I am saying those good times of recognition and reward do not draw me closer to a merciful Lord and do not create any longing for things eternal.

C. S. Lewis offers another perspective: "But if suffering is good, ought it not to be pursued rather than avoided? I answer that suffering is not good in itself. What is good in any painful experience is, for the sufferer, his submission to the will of God, and, for the spectators, the compassion aroused and the acts of mercy to which it leads."[2]

Lewis admits the suffering in itself is not good. It is the fruit or the products yielded from the suffering that have merit. I give testimony God uses suffering to motivate us into submission and to encourage us to acts of compassion.

As the apostle Paul bid farewell to the Ephesian elders, he spoke of his view of suffering and trials:

> And now, compelled by the Spirit, I am going to Jerusalem, not knowing what will happen to me there. I only know that in every city the Holy Spirit warns me that prison and hardships are facing me. However, I consider my life worth nothing to me, if only I may finish the race and complete the task the Lord Jesus has given me—the task of testifying to the gospel of God's grace.
>
> Acts 20:22–24

Paul had to go to Jerusalem in spite of the likely hardship that awaited him; he realized and accepted it was God's purpose that he go. There was work for him to do; there were people he had to touch. He needed to fulfill his mission so that God's eternal plan would be fulfilled.

Paul also put in perspective his likely hardship versus God's purposes. He said his life was "worth nothing" when compared to the task the Lord had for him to complete. Paul put God's purposes ahead of everything else, even his very life. What a struggle it is for us to do the same.

Any Christian parent whose child has died must deal with this very issue. If I accept God is sovereign and nothing happens without His permission, then I must accept He permitted my child's death. He may not have willed it, but He did permit it, and I am led to believe He will use it for His glorious purpose. The writer of the Book of Proverbs tells us, "The LORD works out everything for his own ends" (16:4a).

So, am I as a parent willing or able to give up my child to fulfill God's purposes? This is a critical issue. Its outcome will determine if one is relegated to a life of bitterness or ultimate peace.

I am now able to see how God longs for each of us to be willing to walk into the fire, to sacrifice ourselves, if necessary, to accomplish the task He has planned for us. And it is He who brings us to the point of willingness. This spirit of sacrifice cannot be drummed up within us; we are incapable of overcoming the innate desire to protect self. The true spirit of sacrifice is the product of God's own hand.

In spite of the personal trial he would have to endure, Paul put God's purposes in the number one priority position. Christ did the same thing when He submitted to the authority of the Father and endured the suffering of the cross. He was able to look beyond the moment and see God's greater purpose, sacrificing Himself for the redemption of His people.

Paul spoke of "going to Jerusalem." Jerusalem is a city associated with suffering; it was the end of Christ's earthly ministry, the home of the cross. As Christ spoke of Jerusalem He knew what awaited Him. "Going to Jerusalem" denotes facing hardship and suffering. Am I willing to go to my "Jerusalem"? Christ said, "If anyone would come after me, he must deny himself and take up his cross and follow me," (Matt. 16:24). I must be willing to go to my Jerusalem. I must be willing to endure my suffering when it is part of God's eternal plan.

If I am willing to endure my suffering, God is merciful and will comfort me. His comfort will not come if I resist His authority over me. Resisting His authority over my life leads to bitterness when His plan deviates from mine. At the point of resisting, I am revolting against God and demanding my right to have things my way. In exchange for my submission, He delivers the comfort of His Holy Spirit.

The Necessity of Pain

Most would agree that we do not turn to God; He opens our eyes and turns our hearts to Him. We may have success conforming to His standards and obeying His commands, but can we truly surrender without experiencing pain, suffering, or some form of trial?

It was through Oswald Chambers's writings that it was first suggested to me that some changes are not accomplished without experiencing pain. This was a unique concept to me and I sought confirmation. I found that C. S. Lewis agreed: "Now God, who has made us, knows what we are and that our happiness lies in Him. Yet we will not seek it in Him as long as He leaves us any other resort where it can even plausibly be looked for. While what we call 'our own life' remains agreeable we will not surrender it to Him. What then can God do in our interests but make 'our own life' less agreeable to us, and take away the plausible sources of false happiness."[3]

Suffering has a way of bringing us to the yield point, driving us to our knees, drawing us into total submission. Lewis suggests it may be difficult or unlikely we would totally surrender to our Lord outside the crucible of pain. Through the death of my son and the suffering that followed, I can easily see the means that drove me to surrender more fully to my Lord. There is no question in my mind of my incomplete state of surrender before my son's death. I thought I had yielded myself completely to Christ; however, the incompleteness was obvious after being driven to my knees by my son's death. I must state that my surrender to Christ remains incomplete, but I am more yielded today as a result of Kelly's death than I would have been by any other means.

The Fruit of Suffering

The goal of the Christian life is to be conformed in the image of Christ. This is the process of sanctification. God must work us as the sculptor works metal, as the potter shapes clay. I have become convinced God uses suffering as His most effective tool to conform us in the image of Christ.

M. R. DeHaan captured this thought clearly when he said, "Now, if it is the purpose of the Lord ultimately to make us like the Lord Jesus Christ, that means there must be suffering, pain, and sorrow in our lives. No believer will ever be like Christ without these afflictions, similar to those which Christ experienced so deeply."[4] The question is not, "Do I believe this?" The question is, "Can I accept it?"

To conform us, God must break our will, our internal desire to have things our way. We seek to control our own destiny, to protect our holdings, to make no sacrifice. God will use the circumstances of life to break the back of our strong will, and if we are so foolish as to resist Him, He is more than able to turn up the heat. I am convinced God can humble the hardest heart.

The end product that God desires is the broken spirit, the contrite heart, the submitted believer, the humbled soul. We are to be on our knees at the foot of His throne with our face in the dirt, acknowledging Him as Lord of all, saying, "I am nothing. You are everything." This was the spirit of Jeremiah when he said,

> Do any of the worthless idols of the nations bring rain?
>   Do the skies themselves send down showers?
> No, it is you, O LORD our God.
>   Therefore our hope is in you,
>   for you are the one who does all this.
>
> Jeremiah 14:22

Jeremiah was confessing God was in control. All the other gods of that time were false and unable to affect any change. He was acknowledging God's authority to bring rain, drought, and calamity upon His people.

This was the critical point in my spiritual life. Would I submit to His lordship over my life or seek to maintain control of my own throne?

If I was willing to yield control of my life to Him and submit to His authority and ownership, He would use me for His purposes. If I was unwilling to yield control of my life to Him, my Christian walk and life would be impotent. I would be like a flat tire, which is useless for its purpose.

I began to realize we are of no use to God when we are marching to our own drum. We are only useful to Him when we are marching to His drum. This reminds me of a car. Wouldn't it be interesting if a car had its own will? If this were the case, every time we got behind the wheel, we would be faced with a struggle, trying to drive the car in one direction while the car desired to go in another direction. So it is with us when we are not yielding to Christ's control of our life.

Oswald Chambers said, "As long as you think there is something in you, He cannot choose you because you have ends of your own to serve; But if you have let Him bring you to the end of your self-sufficiency then he can choose you to go with Him to Jerusalem, and that will mean that fulfillment of purposes which he does not discuss with you."[5]

Was I willing to say to my Lord, "My desire in life is to please You"? Was I humbled to the point where I could say, "I do not care what becomes of me as long as You get Your way for Your purposes"?

I realized if I was willing to give up my desires in submission to Christ's desires, then I could go with Him to Jerusalem. The apostle Peter's advice took on new meaning for me: "Humble yourselves, therefore, under God's mighty hand, that he may lift you up in due time" (1 Peter 5:6).

If I humble myself at His feet, He promises to lift me up; not in my time, but in His time; not in the manner I choose, but in the way He chooses; not for my purposes, but for His purposes; not in my strength, but in His strength.

In my weakness His strength abounds. The apostle Paul referred to this when he quoted Jesus: "My grace is sufficient for you, for my power is made perfect in weakness" (2 Cor. 12:9).

Christ's power is never made perfect when we are seeking to accomplish things within our own strength. Paul's response is, "For when I am weak, then I am strong" (2 Cor. 12:10).

It is difficult to understand the paradox. How can we be strong when we are weak? As we get to the end of our rope, we recognize our own shortcomings and weaknesses. All feelings of self-sufficiency are eroded away. God leads us to the conclusion we cannot do it within ourselves; He wants us to realize we must trust in Him absolutely. We are like the rich man whose financial means are slowly drained away until he is reduced to a beggar. No longer the captain of his own destiny, he must rely on someone else. He must seek the good grace and generosity of his fellow man for his next meal. So it must be for us spiritually. Our confidence in our own ability must be destroyed. The cup that was full of self must be slowly poured out until it is empty.

C. S. Lewis reaffirmed this when he said, "The creature's illusion of self-sufficiency must, for the creature's sake, be shattered; and by trouble or fear of trouble on earth, God shatters it unmindful of His glory's diminution."[6]

We must be humbled to the point where we recognize a Holy God is really in charge of everything, and our very lives are grasped in His hands. He decides the outcome. He chooses whether we are happy or sad, rich or poor, healthy or sick, and whether we live a long life or die young.

The fruit of suffering is abdication—the relinquishing of your rights and will to God; the renouncing of your throne and giving it to Jesus Christ with no plans or possibility of resuming the throneship.

For some of us He grabs us by the hand and yanks us to the end of our rope. So it was for me. For others He may be more gentle. The more gentle process reminds me of teaching my dog to sit. I told my dog to sit; when he did not, I gently pushed his bottom down into the sitting position. So it is with God. He wants us to humble ourselves at His throne, yet sometimes, He must gently push us into position.

Once we are humbled, once we have reached the end of self, we are equipped for His service. We are now an empty vessel that has been cleaned out and is ready for refilling with the special drink. At this point we are in the state of weakness that Jesus and the apostle Paul describe in 2 Corinthians 12.

If I will, in that lowly state, cast all my burdens and trials on Jesus, He will lift me up. His strength will arise in me. His power will exude from my very bones. It is now by His power and might, not mine. He now has me firmly grasped in His hand as He wheels me about as an instrument to accomplish His tasks.

This is the vision the apostle Paul captures: "I want to know Christ and the power of his resurrection and the fellowship of sharing in his sufferings, becoming like him in his death, and so, somehow, to attain to the resurrection from the dead" (Phil. 3:10–11).

Above all, Paul wanted to *know* Christ by having that intimate relationship; knowing everything about Him; being like Him in every way possible, even to the point of knowing His sufferings and experiencing the agony of His death so he might be conformed to His likeness and obtain eternal life. Paul knew that all the joys and sorrows of this life were meaningless in the light of the eternal life.

I was now able to say, "Lord, I am Yours, do with my family and me as You please." At this point, I was purged of all fears. I had met death face-to-face and received its worst blow. Nothing in life would be more devastating to me. I was reminded of the passage, "Where, O death, is your victory? Where, O death, is your sting?" (1 Cor. 15:55). Death had indeed lost its sting with me. I was no longer afraid to die.

Previously, I had been one of those people who jumped over the obituary page in the evening newspaper. That was the last page I wanted to read. I now read it nightly; some nights it was the only page I read. I would scan the page passing over anybody who was over fifty years old looking for the young people. Looking for the parent who was now dealing with the same agony as me.

I was now fearless; I could witness to anybody, and I did. I wrote numerous letters telling others of the saving grace of Jesus and sent them to all my relatives and friends. I even sent them to my managers at work whom I had feared offending.

As my cares for self were obliterated, I was filled with a love for Jesus as I had never had before. Scripture opened up for me and reconfirmed to me that Jesus seeks our undivided love. He desires that we have a single-minded, passionate relationship with Him. In John 21 Jesus has an encounter with Peter after the resurrection. Peter and his friends had fished all night to no avail. Jesus spoke to them from the shore and told them to cast their nets to the other side of the boat. When they did this their nets were full. Peter realized who it was and jumped out of the boat and walked to shore. By the time Peter arrived, Jesus had made a fire and suggested they eat some fish. As they were eating, Jesus asked Peter three times, "Do you love me?" Every sermon I had previously heard on this passage emphasized Jesus asked him three times to make up for the fact Peter had denied Christ three times. I now saw something different. I saw the last words of the first question. Jesus said, "Do you truly love me *more than these?*" (John 21:15 italics added).

Who are "these"? I was shown that they were Peter's closest friends. Jesus was asking Peter if his love for Christ exceeded his love for all other earthly beings. Was his love for Christ number one? I was convicted as I realized before Kelly's death I had loved my wife and children more than I loved Jesus. The words of Scripture had penetrated my heart. The Holy Spirit had illumined my mind.

Heaven had a new reality for me. Before, I had an intellectual understanding of heaven, but now it was as real to me as Philadelphia. I know Philadelphia is there. I have been there and I have seen it. It is just up the road. So am I certain of heaven. I know it is there, and I have a strong longing to be there.

Those who have suffered will be used of God, if we let Him. The psalmist says: "He who goes out weeping, carrying seed to sow, will return with songs of joy, carrying sheaves with him" (Ps. 126:6).

If I give testimony to God's grace in bringing me through my suffering, He will use me. If I submit to His authority over my life, He will make me stronger, fill me with His joy, and bear fruit in my life and the lives of others who are impacted by my testimony and witness. I will be permitted to "carry the sheaves with him." I will become a colaborer with Christ, walking and working by His side.

As the apostle Paul approached death he wrote to Timothy: "For I am already being poured out like a drink offering, and the time has come for my departure. I have fought the good fight, I have finished the race, I have kept the faith. Now there is in store for me the crown of righteousness, which the Lord, the righteous Judge, will award to me on that day—and not only to me, but also to all who have longed for his appearing" (2 Tim. 4:6–8).

If we indeed are brought to the point of willingly sacrificing our will to Christ, our life becomes an offering, which we turn over to Christ. He has authority to use us in any manner to accomplish His purposes. Our lives will then be poured out or used by Christ as He pleases. Let each of us say, "Lord, use me for Your purposes. Pour my life out in any way You so choose."

Few people have suffered more than the apostle Paul, yet he was able to say, "I have fought the good fight, I have finished the race, I have kept the faith." No amount of hardship deterred him from his appointed destination; he had dealt with every hole in the road, crossed every river, climbed every mountain to achieve his goal. He was now ready to accept the prize, "the crown of righteousness." It is as if he was saying, "It was all worth it." All his tribulations had resulted in his longing for heaven, the eternal prize that awaits the believer in Christ. Likewise, a crown awaits each of us who persevere until the end.

Our View of God

Our view of God is distorted and must be changed if we are to accept suffering. Since our minds are so opposed to suffering, we have shaped our view of God to exclude it. Why would God permit His children to suffer? Because of our inability to derive a satisfactory answer, we have distorted God's true image. The truth is God does permit His children to suffer in this life.

C. S. Lewis offers an explanation when he says, "We may wish, indeed, that we were of so little account to God that He left us alone to follow our natural impulses—that He would give over trying to train us into something so unlike our natural selves: but once again, we are asking not for more love, but for less."[7]

One of God's major goals is to conform us in His image. We long for the conformation to be accomplished through pleasing and enjoyable events. But change is seldom accomplished through laughter and good times. Change is wrought through hardship and tribulation. Therefore, if God is indeed to conform or reshape our beings, we must endure the painful process.

None of us would permit our own children the joy of total freedom to do and experience all of life's pleasures. This could result in temporary happiness for the child; however, we as parents are keen enough to realize the ultimate havoc and grief of such actions that would create an undisciplined, spoiled child.

God desires to change our natural self, to change us into a being we would not choose if left to our own desires. God is seeking to lead us in a direction that we naturally resist. In this lies God's true love. Not that He seeks to grant us temporary happiness and satisfaction but that He seeks to grant eternal joy and true contentment realized through conformance to His image and in union with His spirit. God is not after the temporary but the eternal; not the short range but the long range.

So it is with the coach of a disciplined athlete. The coach develops a rigorous training program that pushes the athlete to his or her very limits. The athlete may even experience times of resentment as the coach pushes the athlete to excel. However, in the end the athlete is rewarded with the victory and the resentment is turned into elation.

The Eternal Perspective

As I thought about suffering, I was reminded of Kelly's behavior at spanking time. When he was eight or nine, he had an unusual response to spankings. When his behavior was such that he needed a spanking, he would begin to cry as soon as I told him he was going to be spanked. This always amazed me; I would think to myself, *Kelly, why are you crying? You have not even felt any pain.* In actuality, he was anticipating the pain to come.

As a father I could look ahead to the fruit the spanking would yield. I was able to see how this spanking was good for him: The brief pain would bring the desired results in the future. I now am able to see the similarity of this memory with suffering. The apostle Peter comforts us with these words: "In this you greatly rejoice, though now for a little while you may have had to suffer grief in all kinds of trials. These have come so that your faith—of greater worth than gold, which perishes even though refined by fire—may be proved genuine and may result in praise, glory and honor when Jesus Christ is revealed" (1 Peter 1:6–7).

Suffering will only exist for a little while when we view it in the light of eternity. Furthermore, there is a product or fruit from the suffering. God will deliver something wonderful from what appears terrible: All the burdens of this life will disappear when we see Jesus face-to-face. I am holding onto this promise.

It is God's desire we embrace an eternal perspective. The apostle John states: "Do not love the world or anything in the world. If anyone loves the world, the love of the Father is not in him" (1 John 2:15). God wants us to be focused on the eternal world, to look beyond the trials of the moment and see the glory awaiting us in eternity.

Admittedly, this is a difficult concept. How can we extract ourselves and our focus from this world? This world is our reality, and eternity is the unknown. It is like asking one who has never left New York City to desire the farm life of Lancaster, Pennsylvania, when the person has no understanding of what farm life is like. Can we break the chains of identification by ourselves? Can we muster from within the desire to leave this world behind? I think not. I believe God must set us free from the constraints of this world. He is the one who changes our focus, if we will let Him.

Once God sets me free, can I trust Him to keep me afloat or do I attempt to put my feet back on the ground? Therein lies another spiritual battlefront. Satan seeks to draw me back to the things of this world. He encourages me to reconnect the tether; however, I must resist and trust God to deliver His promised eternity.

The disciples were lacking the eternal perspective when Christ told them, "Now I am going to him who sent me, yet none of you asks me, 'Where are you going?' Because I have said these things, you are filled with grief. But I tell you the truth: It is for your good that I am going away. Unless I go away, the Counselor will not come to you; but if I go, I will send him to you" (John 16:5–7).

The disciples were filled with sorrow because Christ was telling them He was going away. They did not realize that joy would follow. They were unable to see beyond the sorrow. So it is with us when we are in the midst of suffering and tribulation. Frequently the burden is overwhelming and we are unable to see beyond it. If the disciples had known what Christ's departure was going to yield, would they have felt differently?

Furthermore, Christ told the disciples it was to their advantage He was going away. I suggest that likewise all suffering and tribulation is to our advantage because God uses it to mold us and conform us to His image. This issue then boils down to trust.

In the midst of my suffering, will I trust God to use it for my ultimate benefit? In the midst of my pain, will I trust God to deliver the future balm that will relieve the sting?

I have become convinced God is able to produce fruit from every tribulation. This is the perspective the disciples failed to have prior to the resurrection. After the resurrection, their joy was complete and all fears were removed. They charged out compelled to speak the truth of Christ's message regardless of personal injury and threat of death.

Sunshine or Sorrow

When everything in your life is going right is it a blessing? Is God showing us favor when the sun is radiantly shining down on us?

Solomon, a man who had experienced every pleasure in life, who sought out and followed every desire man can have, concluded, "sorrow is better than laughter, because a sad face is good for the heart" (Eccles. 7:3). Could it be sorrow provides the true nourishment for the heart, while sunshine and laughter are of no nutritional value? Could it be laughter creates a temporary sweet taste with no substance? Could it be it is through sorrow the heart grows? Could it be that sorrow provides the protein and vitamins making the strong body, while laughter provides the sugar or fat?

Oswald Chambers said, "As long as we get from God everything we ask, we never get to know Him."[8] Is it possible to have an intimate relationship with the Savior outside of the experience of suffering and tribulation? I have become convinced the people blessed of God are those who experience trial and tribulation. This conclusion is the exact opposite of what our worldly minds would seek to conclude. Our nature would tell us the blessed of God are those whose lives are grand, free from hardship. However, I suggest the blessed of God are those who have an intimate relationship with Christ, those who "know" Him.

Are we willing or able to give up the sunshine to endure the storm? As we look to nature, we are able to see where constant sunshine delivers a parched ground while the storm brings the rain that yields growth and an abundance of fruit. Is it so in our spiritual lives? I suggest it is. Am I willing to weather the storm to "know" Him?

God is merciful and does provide respites from the hardships of life. In fact, we may have lengthy periods when God's grace abounds. As I examine my life I can see God's preparation time. He had prepared Patty and me to cope with the suffering prior to our son's death. He had grounded us in our faith and taken us through smaller trials so that our faith was strengthened for the greater ordeal. Could it be God lets us fill our storehouse with water before the drought?

I have asked myself repeatedly, "Where would I be spiritually if Kelly had not died?" I have even gone through the mental exercise of asking what would I do if God offered to bring back my son in exchange for how He has changed the lives of my wife, son, daughter, and self. Do I value how He has changed my family and all He has taught me more than my longing for my son? Would I give up all I have learned to have my son back in this life? This becomes a very difficult question, but I am hopeful I could maintain the eternal perspective and hold onto God's teachings, accepting that I will see my son soon in eternity.

I readily confess I have been a stubborn student—one who has not learned lessons easily and who has sought to teach himself. I admit it is doubtful I would have volunteered to be conformed in the manner God has chosen. However, I can see how God has used my son's death to teach my family and me lessons we would not have learned otherwise.

A Perspective on Life

There is coming a time when everything we value in this life will be meaningless. The prophet Isaiah describes that time as follows:

> The arrogance of man will be brought low
>   and the pride of men humbled;
> the LORD alone will be exalted in that day,
>   and the idols will totally disappear.
>
> Men will flee to caves in the rocks
>   and to holes in the ground
> from dread of the LORD
>   and the splendor of his majesty,
>   when he rises to shake the earth.
> In that day men will throw away
>   to the rodents and bats
> their idols of silver and idols of gold,
>   which they made to worship.
> They will flee to caverns in the rocks
>   and to the overhanging crags
> from dread of the LORD
>   and the splendor of his majesty,
>   when he rises to shake the earth.
>
> Stop trusting in man,
>   who has but a breath in his nostrils.
> Of what account is he?
>
> Isaiah 2:17–22

We are destined to be humbled when each item in our value system is measured against the yardstick of God. Do we value the right things? Is our priority system in the right order?

I remember watching the low-budget Japanese monster movies when I was a teenager. Movie after movie depicted the fright—as the monster approached, everybody dropped their belongings, ceased their current activities, and ran for their lives. Nothing mattered at the moment but to escape the monster.

So it will be when God's judgment approaches, "men will flee to caves in the rocks and to holes in the ground."

All possessions will be left behind; all the money in the world will be useless.

So it is also at the moment of death; nothing else matters. No amount of money can buy your way out. All possessions are left behind. Just as man will flee from God's judgment so man flees from death. We hide from it by seeking the caves and holes of this world, but there is no escape from it. It persists and stalks each of us down in due time. Yet does this reality cause us to reevaluate our focus and value system? Most would say no. We continue to behave as if this world is the end-all. We continue to place our priorities on the things of this life and seem to ignore the approaching end.

If we measured things by their eternal rather than worldly value, wouldn't we be less disillusioned and frustrated by the failures of this life? Wouldn't we view death in a different way? Wouldn't we fear it less?

Dear Lord, help me to stay focused on You. Help me to think of Kelly surrounded by Your glory. These thoughts draw me away from the images of his death. May I be reminded of the perfection he now shares with You. May I see him basking in the contentment and joy of Your love. Dear Lord, give me patience to wait on You. Help me to stay focused on my remaining earthly responsibilities as I am drawn to thoughts of heaven.

Is it possible, dear Lord, to desire to be in both places? Part of me remains on earth while part of me awaits that reunion in heaven. The separation seems so great, yet I must be mindful that the time is short. Short, dear Lord, from Your perspective and short from Kelly's, even though to me the seconds seem as years.

With sadness and sorrow comes new knowledge. I have a new appreciation of the separation You felt as Your Son Jesus hung on the cross. May I look forward and anticipate the joyful reunion You had when Jesus returned to His heavenly throne.

May 28

Chapter 6

My Response

Why Did Kelly Have to Die?

Can I blame my son's death on God? The Bible presents numerous reasons why bad things happen to God's people. The obvious reason and the one most people think of first is discipline. Is it true God disciplines His children? According to the Book of Hebrews it is: "And you have forgotten that word of encouragement that addresses you as sons: 'My son, do not make light of the Lord's discipline, and do not lose heart when he rebukes you, because the Lord disciplines those he loves, and he punishes everyone he accepts as a son'" (Heb. 12:5–6).

Was there sin in my life for which I was being punished? I did not feel God was punishing me. God does chastise His children, but I did not feel God's wrath, nor were there any other signs to suggest He was angry with me.

God lets Satan have free reign with some as He did with Job. Job was a righteous man, undeserving of discipline. "Then the LORD said to Satan, 'Have you considered my servant Job? There is no one on earth like him; he is blameless and upright, a man who fears God and shuns evil'" (Job 1:8). God permitted Satan's testing of Job. Job's children were killed and he was stripped of his possessions. His physical well-being was attacked as he was covered by sores. All this was unjustified and unfair from our worldly perspective. Yet God used it for His purposes.

Sometimes God permits infirmity so His grace may be displayed in a person's life. This is evident in some people who have disabilities as we observe how they daily submit to God and hold no bitterness for their condition. Other times infirmity is present so God may display His healing power. Such was the case with Lazarus's death. God permitted the tragic event so He would be glorified through Christ's response to the death. Christ knew Lazarus was dying and yet did not move to heal him because He desired the greater miracle. Jesus stayed on two more days so that Lazarus would die. Jesus had no intention of healing Lazarus; He procrastinated His visit so death would overcome. This is reaffirmed when Jesus said to his disciples, "Lazarus is dead, and for your sake I am glad I was not there, so that you may believe. But let us go to him" (John 11:14–15).

Jesus could have healed Lazarus, but He chose not to so He could perform the greater miracle of bringing Lazarus back from the dead. It is very revealing when Jesus was confronted by Mary's and the others' weeping. His response was to weep too. Jesus knew He was going to bring Lazarus back, but He did not let this fact interfere with His sharing in the grief. Jesus was overcome with compassion when He saw and felt the grief of Mary and the others.

Jesus proceeded to raise up Lazarus, and this miracle caused many to believe. In John 11:45 we read, "Therefore many of the Jews who had come to visit Mary, and had seen what Jesus did, put their faith in him." This passage shows how Jesus used a tragic event to glorify Himself.

Lazarus's death was indeed tragic and caused much sorrow. Jesus could have healed Lazarus, but He chose to wait to perform the greater work.

Can we bear the tragedy of the moment as we wait for Christ to perform the greater miracle? Can we look beyond the darkness of the hour to the light ahead? Can we trust God to use our suffering to accomplish a greater event?

Why did my son have to die? Did God cause it or did He permit it? Must I know the reason? How long must I struggle to find the answers to these questions?

I remember reading a book in which death was compared to a vehicle traveling from one point to another. The book suggested the means of travel was irrelevant. The important point was arriving at your destination, not the mode of transportation.

Should I take time and energy to try to understand why my son died and who caused his death? Would I ever be able to find those answers? I concluded I would never understand why he had to die. I also concluded it did not matter if God caused my son to die or if He just permitted his death. None of this reasoning would ever bring my son back. So, I gave it up. I accepted I would not have those answers while on this earth and I must focus on trying to understand what I must do in response to my son's death. The act was done. The hour had passed. How could I go forward? That was the overriding issue.

What Are Our Rights?

The United States Constitution says we are created with certain inalienable rights, one being the pursuit of happiness. As United States citizens, do we have the right to happiness? Is that one of our God-given freedoms? Our nature would say yes! We have the right to enjoy life and be happy!

The apostle Paul says, "You are not your own; you were bought at a price" (1 Cor. 6:19–20). This declaration makes me mindful of the master/slave relationship. Not one in which the master oppresses or forces allegiance, but one in which the master willingly gives of himself for the benefit of the slave. It is a sacrificial relationship that evokes love for the master and willing obedience by the slave. In the master/slave relationship the slave has no rights except those given by the master. The psalmist says, "As the eyes of slaves look to the hand of their master, . . . so our eyes look to the LORD our God" (Ps. 123:2).

The master/slave relationship parallels our relationship with Jesus. Christ has purchased us, redeemed us through the sacrifice of His body. As Paul said, He has bought us. Through the sacrifice of Himself for His people Christ offers the lordship of a merciful master in exchange for our submission to Him.

Scripture also speaks of God's perfect plan. Was there a purpose in Christ coming to this earth and becoming man? Did God know Christ would be crucified? Did God realize through Christ's sacrifice, man would be redeemed from eternal damnation? YES, YES, YES. . . . God does have a plan that He is working out. A plan that not only addresses the generalities of His creation, but that is individualized for each of us and includes every detail of our lives.

I have a plan for my life. I have dreams for my children. I am saving money for my children's college education and money for that dream vacation. I have longings and desires for things I plan to accomplish. As an American I would even claim the right to have such plans.

So what does one do when those plans are shattered? What does one do when the child who had so much potential, was so gifted, had so many good times ahead, dies? Have your rights been violated? Can I give up my rights to have life the way I want it or is that asking too much? Would a loving God expect me to willingly give up my son? Is it possible God would require me to make such a sacrifice?

Is God sovereign? Merriam Webster's Collegiate Dictionary describes sovereign as one who is "possessed of supreme power, absolute, having undisputed ascendancy." I am mindful of God's discourse with Job. "Where were you when I laid the earth's foundation? . . . Have you ever given orders to the morning, or shown the dawn its place?" (Job 38:4, 12).

God is the creator, and we are the creatures. God has made us and has complete dominion over us. Who are we to make demands of God? Who are we to object when life does not fit our plan?

What did Jesus Christ say when He was faced with the crucifixion, a plan that was not to His liking? "Father, if you are willing, take this cup from me" (Luke 22:42a). If the cup was not to be passed by, He was willing to submit to the authority of the Father. "Yet, not my will, but yours be done" (Luke 22:42b). Are we to submit to the Father's sovereign will when we don't approve of the plan?

Can I yield ownership of myself, of my family, of my life's desires to Christ? Can I, the slave, submit to the Master? Can I yield to the Master's desires ahead of my own desires?

What do we do when yielding requires accepting heartbreak? Oswald Chambers provided an answer when he said, "Why shouldn't we go through heartbreaks? Through these doorways God is opening up ways of fellowship with His Son. If through a broken heart, God can bring His purposes to pass in the world, then thank Him for breaking your heart."[1]

Chambers equates heartbreak to fellowship with Christ. Can we have true fellowship with Christ outside of the broken heart? Do I value fellowship with Christ more than my desire to keep my heart whole? Am I willing to experience a broken heart if it means my fellowship with Christ is more complete? Is it a fair exchange?

Chambers further suggests I should willingly sacrifice my heart for the fulfillment of God's purposes. If the events break my heart, yet God uses those events for His purposes, I am challenged to accept His Holy purposes and give up my interests. God's expectation is for me to give up my rights to have things my way. Who am I to question God's motives? "The LORD does whatever pleases him, in the heavens and on the earth, in the seas and all their depths" (Ps. 135:6). Need He seek my approval before He proceeds?

As the psalmist concludes, God is in control. It is not I who decides my fate. As with the wayward child, I must submit to the Father's rule. I must submit to His action and permissive will even when my body and will revolt against Him. In the end, He is the authority.

Jeremiah the prophet reaffirmed this when he said, "I know, O LORD, that a man's life is not his own; it is not for man to direct his steps. Correct me, LORD, but only with justice—not in your anger, lest you reduce me to nothing" (Jer. 10:23–24).

God has complete dominion over us, and He alone has the "right" to control the events of our lives, even the ultimate event of reducing me to nothing.

The apostle Paul said, "I have been crucified with Christ and I no longer live, but Christ lives in me" (Gal. 2:20). Paul's life, his will, his rights, are no more; he has yielded himself to Christ. Christ now has dominion or rule over Paul. I have discovered it is this yielding of self that sets the believer free. It is this yielding of self that releases me to be the instrument of God controlled by the Spirit. This is the process of "dying to self."

Can I Trust God Fully?

In the midst of suffering, can I trust God? When my hopes have been dashed on the rocks, can I be assured God will see me through the trial? When I am at the bottom of the pit, can I trust God to lift me out? Can I believe God loves me when all worldly evidence says no? These are questions I had to deal with individually. No amount of discussion with someone else was going to persuade me to trust God. I had to reach out in faith and choose to trust Him even when there was zero evidence or reason to do such. I have learned God wants me to trust Him even when there is every reason not to trust Him. The prophet Isaiah says, "You will keep in perfect peace him whose mind is steadfast, because he trusts in you" (26:3).

I must wait for God, for He controls and directs my life. I have learned that He is in control, not me. Life will be lived out not as I have planned but as He has planned. "I wait for the LORD, my soul waits, and in his word I put my hope" (Ps. 130:5).

As I long to be with Him, I must wait until His appointed time. I must hold onto His promises of deliverance and of eternal life. These are documented in His Word and are my hope, a hope rooted in the trust that God will deliver what He promises.

Even Jesus Christ, the man, was faced with trusting God the Father in the midst of his suffering. "Although he was a son, he learned obedience from what he suffered" (Heb. 5:8). If God the Father was unwilling to spare His own Son the trial of suffering, why should I expect Him to spare me? And therefore, since He has not spared me, is that grounds to not trust Him? In fact, is the corollary true? Since He has not spared me from suffering, is it a sign of my adoption as His son?

The apostle Peter provided us with a good example of trusting God. In Matthew 14 we read: "When the disciples saw him walking on the lake, they were terrified. 'It's a ghost,' they said, and cried out in fear. But Jesus immediately said to them: 'Take courage! It is I. Don't be afraid.' 'Lord, if it's you,' Peter replied, 'tell me to come to you on the water.' 'Come,' he said. Then Peter got down out of the boat, walked on the water and came toward Jesus" (26–29).

The disciples were greatly afraid for two reasons: (1) the boat was being "buffeted by the waves," and (2) they thought they were seeing a ghost. This setting was further disturbing to the disciples because Jesus was walking on water—a completely unnatural event. Peter, even though he was scared and unsure, ventured outside of his world, offering to walk on water as well. Now comes the trust when Jesus says, "Come." Who of us would attempt to step out on the water in rough seas? When we are at the end of our rope and the only remaining option is to trust Christ, will we step out? This is the example Peter provided. The seas were rough and Jesus said, "Come." At this point Peter's only reason to step out of the boat was belief that Christ would provide the means. All evidence from this world said, "No! Don't do it." Yet Peter trusted Christ to overcome all of nature's laws. He stepped out in faith.

We too must step out in faith to believe the impossible or to trust Christ to see us through a situation that has no reasonable path, no way out. Can we trust Christ when there is no earthly alternative or way of dealing with our specific situation? Christ desires to bring each one of us to the point where there is no other alternative but to trust Him.

Have you ever participated in the exercise of falling back into someone's arms? This scary test involves a great deal of trust in the person who is slated to catch you. So it is with Christ. He desires for each of us to fall back into His arms. Can we trust Him to catch us?

Is the Lesson Too Difficult?

Many times, when laden with grief, I have felt my loss was too much to handle. I have felt this lesson, which I was being forced to learn, was too difficult. One day as I was reading the Book of John the Spirit spoke to me.

After Jesus fed the five thousand, He and the disciples crossed the Sea of Galilee to Capernaum. It was during this crossing at night that Jesus walked on water. When they arrived at Capernaum Jesus began to teach. At one point Jesus said, "I tell you the truth, unless you eat the flesh of the Son of Man and drink his blood, you have no life in you. Whoever eats my flesh and drinks my blood has eternal life, and I will raise him up at the last day" (John 6:53–54). Some people's response to this difficult teaching was to resist the message: "This is a hard teaching. Who can accept it?" (John 6:60). As a result many departed. "From this time many of his disciples turned back and no longer followed him" (John 6:66).

Often when we are faced with difficult teachings, we too may choose to say, "This teaching is too hard to accept." So it is with grief. Many times I have had this very thought.

Upon seeing many depart, Jesus turned to the Twelve and asked, "You do not want to leave too, do you?" (John 6:67).

It was as if Jesus was aiming this question directly at me. Was the lesson I was being forced to learn too difficult? Would I too depart from Him? As I read on I was able to understand the apostle Peter's response. "Lord, to whom shall we go? You have the words of eternal life" (John 6:68).

In my grief was there anywhere else to go? Was there anyone else to turn to? Were there any other acceptable answers? Did anyone else have a solution? Could anyone else take away my pain? Could anyone else bring back my son? I was brought to the same point as Peter. Only the Lord Jesus has the answers. I was going to trust in Him and believe God was executing His perfect plan.

Dr. Larry Crabb illustrates and confirms my learning experience. As God breaks us into submission and reveals

His truth, our questions and perspectives change. "When the lights go out, when our dreams shatter and there's no way to piece them back together, that's when our questions are most likely to change. No longer do we ask, 'Am I right?' We realize we can't be right enough to make things happen as we want. Instead we ask, 'Whom do I trust?'"[2]

Several months after Kelly's death Patty and I were invited to a friend's house for brunch with a group of other couples. I was still feeling rather unsociable, but I went anyway. As I was standing with a group of men, one father began to share the difficulty he was having because his twenty-year-old daughter had moved out of the home. He said, "I am devastated." I bit my tongue and chose to say nothing even though I wanted to get in his face and explain to him what real devastation was. I was rather angry at the moment.

Later, God showed me a different perspective. My son's death was my number one problem; it was the most difficult thing in my life. For the other father, his daughter's move away from the home was his number one problem. In my opinion, his problem was insignificant compared to mine. My reaction was, "Twenty-year-old daughters are supposed to move out of the home." In reality, the significance of my number one problem did not diminish his. His problem was the most difficult issue in his life at that moment, and I had to recognize it as such. I could not impose my problem on him. I was much more tolerant of others after learning this lesson. God deals with each one of us uniquely. He chooses the lessons we must learn and ultimately controls all the events in our life.

What matters in life, dear Lord? I know it is not wealth, nor power, nor position; it is not new cars or beautiful homes; it is not a promotion or an award; it is not success; it is not health; it is not security; it is not happiness or length of life.

For all these things, dear Lord, come and go, are enjoyed by the undeserving and are stripped away from all of us in time.

Only love is eternal! For I shall take that with me when I pass from this life and realize its fullness when I see Your face.

May 16

The Struggle Continues

The Grief Process

Grieving is very personal. Each person approaches it differently, and each one follows his or her own time line. Psychologists propose there are defined steps a grieving person follows. I concur there are common elements, but it has been my experience some of those steps are bypassed by some people. There is one thing in common, however: Grief cannot be avoided. People may delay it or temporarily go around it, but they are always brought back to it. If they ignore the death or pretend it did not happen, they are only procrastinating dealing with the agony.

I found that if I let my emotions flow, the process moved forward. It was even beneficial doing things to help the emotions flow. I listened to those special songs that reminded me of Kelly. I looked at the family picture album.

I read old letters. I talked to others about Kelly. I acknowledged I felt terrible. I concluded all these feelings were okay; feeling terrible is the normal reaction to death.

Since everyone grieves uniquely, Patty and I learned to give each other space to be different. We actually went through a lengthy period where we had very low expectations of each other. She was not demanding of me, and I was not demanding of her. We were both willing to accept survival rather than have high expectations of each other. Patty was very supportive and tolerant of my moody behavior.

One person may laugh at a memory that evokes tears in another. One may wish to be alone while another desires to be surrounded by many people. This can be especially difficult for husbands and wives who have lost a child. It is almost impossible for one grieving person to comfort another grieving person. Putting that burden on a spouse almost always results in disaster.

A Lifelong Journey

Grief is a lifelong journey. It is not something one experiences for six months and then moves on. There is no set recuperation period. Grief is not an illness that occupies a few days and is then over. It encompasses peaks and valleys that are very sharp and very close at first. The pointedness of the peaks diminishes and the depth of the valleys lessens with time; but they do not disappear.

Each individual's journey is different. It was my experience that the pointedness of my pain did not begin to diminish until three years after my son's death. I felt little relief during the first three years, but I did begin to feel healing after that time.

The more pain one lets oneself experience, the faster the healing. The more one procrastinates and avoids the pain, the slower the healing. This is sometimes described as "leaning into the pain." One must walk through the pain and not around it. In my opinion, if one's nature permits, it is better to deal with a little pain each day, rather than ignore it for long periods of time.

Grief is not something one can schedule. It can creep up quickly at unexpected times and catch one by surprise. It may be prompted by a word, a memory, a song, or any other item which creates a brief thought or remembrance. One can be laughing at one moment and crying at the next. There is no anticipation of grief.

Approximately five years after Kelly's death, I went on a business trip to England for one week. The trip was very enjoyable and busy. It was almost nonstop, and I visited and saw many new things. However, when I came back home I went into a deep depression that lasted almost a month. It later became obvious to me that the trip to England was a diversion from reality. I had briefly escaped the fact of Kelly's death. I had entered a dream world for a time but upon my return was again faced with the reality of my son's death. It had not gone away; it was merely placed on the shelf for a brief time. The first Sunday back I cried all the way to church and through half of the worship service. My sense of loss was just as fresh as it had been five years before.

Shane's Struggle

Shane was sixteen when Kelly died. He ignored his grief and pretended it did not exist. He even became angry when the subject was mentioned. Total avoidance can only describe his approach to his brother's death.

Two and one half years after Kelly died, Shane was now eighteen and headed off to a small Christian college in Georgia. I knew he was going to get homesick and I had told him in advance he was probably going to call, begging me to come and get him. I told him I was going to say no.

The process of taking Shane away to school and leaving him there was very difficult for all of us. By the fourth week Patty and I knew Shane was having great difficulty. We began to speak to him almost daily by phone encouraging him to stay one more day. He told us he was spending time in his room crying in between classes. By the fifth week we were speaking to him twice daily by phone. He told me there were other students who were homesick too; but it was different for him.

We began to realize Shane was dealing with more than the usual homesickness. He had stuffed many of the feelings regarding Kelly's death, and these were now surfacing. He had postponed the grieving process and the homesickness had acted as a stimulus to bring him back to it. We concluded it would be best for him to be back home where we could support him as he worked through his feelings. So on a Thursday night at 6:00 P.M. Patty and I departed from our home in Elkton, Maryland, and headed south. We arrived at the school at 5:30 the next morning after driving all night. Not wanting to wake up the dorm, we stayed in the car until 6:00 A.M. We had the car loaded by 7:00 A.M. and headed back up north arriving home at 8:00 that evening. Patty and I had spent twenty-six consecutive hours in the old family wagon, which had over 140,000 miles. We were so thankful to our Lord for having made the trip with no problems.

On the way home Shane told us he thought he was getting away from his grief by going away to school, and he thought he would be able to get on with his life. However, he soon realized he could not run away. Before leaving for school, he had avoided his brother's death, but upon his return home he faced reality. His brother had indeed died, and Shane was now able to cry and let the emotions flow. He decided to move into Kelly's old bedroom, and he gathered all the memorabilia he could find, putting up pictures, hanging up old baseball mitts, and doing other things that reminded him of his brother. This was real progress for him.

Patty and I later found out Shane had only let himself experience a little grief. Two years later, when he was twenty, he went into severe depression. We were beginning to see the pattern we had heard about four years before. It appears children can only deal with small amounts of grief, a little at a time. As they mature they deal with different aspects of grief and experience different levels of emotion. At sixteen Shane chose to deal with very little grief. At eighteen he experienced another level of emotion, and now at twenty he was dealing with a new set of emotions. The journey was very real to Shane. His brother's death was still a very real part of his life and a continuing struggle.

A Remnant of Pain

There is an element within me that wishes to hold onto my pain. I do not want to heal completely in this life. I do not want all my pain to go away. I want to hold onto a remnant of pain, so that I do not forget my son. There is a fear of letting go of his memory and a belief that as long as I feel pain I will not forget him.

There is a spiritual aspect to this as well. Through Kelly's death I was driven to my knees spiritually. I was humbled as I had never been humbled before, and I experienced the peace of totally resting in the arms of my Lord. There is a fear that someday those feelings of self-sufficiency that were so strong before my son died will return. A fear I will get up off my knees and again seek to live life within my own strength. Therefore, I often pray, "Lord, do whatever you must to keep me on my knees." This is a bold prayer, because it is soliciting more suffering. I have on occasion said, "If you want to be close to Jesus, pray for suffering."

Being immersed in suffering will bring you into His presence faster than anything else I know.

Dr. Larry Crabb concurs with my conclusion; he says, "Do I love him so deeply that I welcome additional suffering that might draw my soul closer to him? Will I pay any price to know him well?"[1] This is another of life's dilemmas, I want to know Him, but am I willing to endure the pain to know Him better?

The Magnitude of Grief

When asking about the death of your child, people will often ask whether you have other children. When you answer yes, their next question is, "How many?" When I say, "Two," their response often minimizes my grief. It is as if my other two children somehow compensate for the death. In reality, the fact that I have two other children in no way minimizes my grief or makes up for the death of the other child.

A similar response is often given with the death of elderly people. When you tell someone your mother has died, people will frequently ask, "How old was she?" If your response is "seventy" or "eighty," the person tends to minimize your grief. The fact is, just because your mother was older, in no way will you miss her less, nor will your grief be minimized. The death of a loved one creates a void that in most cases is not filled by any other person.

Certainly, the death of a young person is more tragic than the death of an older person who has lived a full life. However, we must be sensitive to not let the degree of the tragedy impact how we relate to the griever. A less tragic death does not translate to experiencing less grief.

These same principles apply to the circumstances surrounding the death. Because a child dies in a car wreck while driving under the influence of alcohol does not mean that the mother of that child will grieve any less than the mother whose child was killed by another driver. The circumstances of the death do not impact the magnitude of the grief.

Death is death and grief is grief, regardless of age or circumstances.

All That Matters

What is important today can be totally insignificant tomorrow. As parents we worry so much about our children. We worry about their grades, their friends, their clothes, their teeth; it goes on and on. Yet, are those items really important?

At the moment we found our son dead, only one thing in all of life mattered. Did he know Jesus Christ as his Lord and Savior? Was he now in heaven? Did he have eternal life and, therefore, would I see him again? All the other things were insignificant. And yet, as I think back to how much effort and energy we put into the other things, I am reminded of how much I had worried about things that in the end have no bearing on the outcome. When the bottom line is drawn, these other issues will be irrelevant.

By God's grace, Kelly had come to know the saving grace of Jesus Christ. I have the evidence in his very own handwriting. What guilt would I feel if I did not know my son's spiritual condition? I thought back to all the things Patty and I did to lead our children to Christ. We took them to church, we sent them to a Christian school, we read them Bible stories, we spoke of Christ and our faith at home, we had fellowship with other believers who had children of our children's age, and we prayed at home. If I did not have the confidence Kelly was in heaven, would I feel guilty that I had not done enough? Most parents do not plan on their children dying and, therefore, do not have a sense of urgency about this issue. But I can see now my child's salvation was the most important issue I as a parent would face.

And so, I appeal to you, are you doing everything in your power, everything within your means, to lead your child to Christ? Are you using every opportunity, everything at your access, every possible alternative to expose your child to the saving grace of Jesus Christ? Is it your most important responsibility? Do you see it as your most important mission in life? There may come a time as it did for me, where it is the only thing that matters. All other things fade away.

A Changing Value System

Death reorders your entire life, especially your value system.

As I listen to others' conversation, I am amazed at their value system. I become angry as I hear parents talk about the problems their children cause them. Because, for the most part, those so called problems or aggravations are minor; yet often these problems are spoken of as major. As I hear parents speak of this and that, I think how I would welcome the opportunity to deal with those problems with my son. If given a second chance, I would welcome almost any difficulty my son would bring forward, if only he were alive.

We have friends whose son had a stroke at birth and is handicapped. Upon seeing him, I was always reminded how fortunate I was to have three healthy children. I was always thankful none of my children were handicapped, thankful I did not have to deal with such a burden. After Kelly died, I longed to have him back, even if he was handicapped. I thought about these parents and was envious they had a son I did not have. Even though their son was handicapped, they could still talk to him, they could hold him, they could touch him, smell him, and feel his warmth. I wish I could speak to every parent who has a handicapped child for I know they experience great frustration; however, if only they could have my perspective. If only they could realize how I have envied them at times and have longed to have my child back even if he was handicapped. I realize this is indeed a selfish perspective, and I admit my view moderates with my emotions and the extent of my grief.

When I returned to work, I would be in meetings and see with what vigor people would argue over issues. And yet, I could not see the importance of those issues. I would ask myself, "What's the big deal?" I did not have the patience to belabor small points. Business issues seemed so meaningless compared to eternal issues. It was even more obvious to me how little interest people had for eternal issues compared to the day-to-day pressing need of business. I felt like screaming out to those people, "Don't you realize you are going to be held accountable before a Holy God? Don't you realize you are going to die someday and meet your Maker face-to-face?" I had to remind myself we are blind to spiritual things until the Lord opens our eyes.

True Joy

I have always been somewhat offended with the idea Christians should smile all the time. This concept is often played out in church services by pastors as they chastise the congregation for looking gloomy and encourage them to smile. I believe this is a result of not understanding the difference between joy and happiness. Smiling or laughing is a characteristic of happiness not necessarily joy.

Frequently during worship services as I am singing hymns and praises I am overcome with emotion. As I reflect on my Lord and my desire to be with Him, the tears flow. Therefore, it has been my experience when I am filled with joy and love for my Lord, I am not laughing or smiling, but, in fact, I am crying. Joy is peace that passes understanding. Joy is confidence and trust in Jesus and His forgiveness, which can exist in the face of tragedy and trial. Joy is the abiding peace and hope in the awaiting eternal life that no one can take away or destroy. No person or set of circumstances can separate me from the love of Christ. Therefore, even in the crucible of pain I can have joy. Even in agony, the love of Christ can reach out and touch me, consoling my aching heart and filling me with His joy. My greatest moments of joy have been in the midst of tears when I am longing to be with my Master and feeling the warmth of His arms surrounding me. There is a song by Don Moen that captures my feeling; the first stanza reads:

> I just want to be where You are
> Dwelling daily in Your presence
> I don't want to worship from afar
> Draw me near to where You are.[2]

I long to be in the presence of the Lord Jesus, to lay at His feet and worship Him.

A Longing for Christ

As a result of my grief, I have sought out people who have had a similar experience. I have read many books on grief, and, as I read, I seek the pearl of wisdom. So it was when I read C. S. Lewis's *A Grief Observed*. In this book the author shares his agony over the death of his wife from cancer. He shares the hopelessness and the loneliness of grief. He repeatedly shares his longing to see his wife whom he refers to as "H." in his writings. Page after page I read, finding no pearl.

Finally, I found the pearl when C. S. Lewis realizes, "Lord, are these your real terms? Can I meet H. again only if I learn to love you so much that I don't care whether I meet her or not?"[3] Through all his lamenting he is brought to the point of seeing his need to love Jesus foremost, even more than his wife. This was the pearl. This was the one sentence worthy of reading the entire book.

I was able to see the similarity of our journeys. When Kelly first died, I longed for heaven. Not so much to be with my Savior, but more so to be with my son and to leave behind the heartache of this life. However, as time passed, the Lord transformed this longing to be with my son into a desire to be with Him. I now long for heaven, to lie down at the feet of my Savior, and to rest in His peace. While I still long to see my son, I long to see Jesus more.

Why is it, Lord, that my longing for heaven seems so foreign to others? As Your Word says, "No eye as seen, no ear has heard, no mind has conceived, what God has prepared for those that love him." Your Word tells us that heaven is a glorious place free from all of earth's trials. If we believe this, why does my longing seem so strange to some, as if unnatural? Have I answered my own question? It is our nature to love this world. It is not our nature to seek Your face. It is our nature to fear the unknown and to hold onto the security blankets of this life. I have sought comfort in knowing that Kelly is with You, in believing that heaven is far better than this world. Has my intensity of thought distorted my thinking or have You given me a measure of grace?

Dear Lord, I want it to be glorious. I want to think of death as only a tunnel through which we pass. I want to trust in You. Even when that requires accepting my son's death.

June 11

Chapter *8*

Reaching Out
to Others

Death—The Untouchable Subject

Death is something few people care to discuss. Even the closest of friends may avoid the subject. Relatives do not know what to say to one another when a family member dies.

When I returned to work after Kelly died, I expected certain people to be the first ones to come up to me; they never came. People I met during the day might squeak out a small, quiet, "I'm sorry." Seldom was more than a brief condolence expressed. I wanted to talk about Kelly. I wanted to tell someone all the intimate details of his death. I wanted to share my pain. No one asked!

There is a commonly held view that says, "I don't want to mention the death to my friend, because I do not want to cause him more grief." If this is true of most people, it is another one of life's great paradoxes, because quite the contrary was true for me. As I grieved over Kelly, I wanted to talk about him. I wanted to be reminded of him. I wanted to talk about the tragic events that had happened. Yet, it was as if no one would listen. Few people cared to ask or give me the opportunity to share my grief.

Is it possible the commonly held view mentioned above is false? Could it be the real reason for not talking about death is to protect the consoler? May the consoler's actual feelings be, "I don't know what to say. I feel inadequate. It makes me uncomfortable. I don't want to be reminded of this bad experience. I don't want to be reminded of my own mortality"?

For the most part, death is ignored. It has become the untouchable subject. People either pretend it does not exist or believe it is something that will never impact them.

Agony Relived

Two and one half years after Kelly died we received a 1:30 A.M. phone call from our pastor's brother-in-law. David said, "Jehu, Mark died tonight in a car accident." Mark was our pastor's youngest son, a sixteen-year-old who had played basketball with Shane. The feeling of helplessness rolled over me. I woke Patty to tell her the news only to hear her gasp in agony. We proceeded to get dressed and head for the hospital. When we arrived there our pastor and his wife had already left and returned home. We then went to their home to find a small gathering of people already there.

The comforters were there, but there was no comfort to give. Everyone looked as if in a trance. Little was being said; the wailing and agony overpowered all else. Only Patty and I knew their pain. No one else who was there knew the loss of a child. They could only mildly relate to the pain from a distance.

There were no words to say, no wisdom to share, only tears. We knew the pain could not be taken away. There was no relief now, nor would there be for months and years to come. Our hearts went out to them, for we knew of the hard road ahead.

I could only give them a few simple words of encouragement that I typed up and placed on their refrigerator door several days later.

Jehu's Rules for Grieving

1. Lay yourself at Jesus' feet. Totally surrender everything to Him. Ask Him for help to get out of bed each morning.
2. Cry, cry, and cry some more. It is your best means of releasing pain.
3. Support each other, giving each one space to grieve as they wish. Each person handles it differently.

The next day my family realized how far the Lord had taken us in the last two years. We had not been able to see our progress until we relived those first few hours with our pastor's family. We had a retaste of the bitter agony. I remembered the words of another father whose daughter had died. He told me shortly after Kelly's death it would get better with time, and I responded, "No! It will never get better." It was now evident to me that Jesus Christ stills works miracles and my family was the recipient of His healing power. It was confirmed He can still bring healing to a broken heart.

In the months that followed I watched our pastor's family walk down a path similar to my family's. It was different for them, because each one responds uniquely; however, they had to learn the same lessons. They had to deal with the same issues. I could not take away their pain, nor could I usher them through the tough times. They had to go through it alone leaning only on God. I could stand on the sidelines and offer encouragement. I could offer to bind their wounds, but I could not fight the battle for them. God would see them through the trial, teaching them the lessons He chose and bringing them His healing in His time.

Reaching Out to Kelly's Friends

Kelly and our pastor's son, Mark, went to the same Christian school. The students at this school had now experienced the death of three of their classmates within a two-and-one-half-year period, for another fifteen-year-old classmate died in the car accident with Mark.

I felt a calling to go and speak to these young people, to offer them encouragement and to share with them what God was teaching me. So I called the school's principal and asked if I could speak at one of the weekly chapel services.

On January 7, 1994, I shared the following five points:

1. If you are one of God's people, you will have trials, trials that are life changing: marital problems, divorce, death of a loved one, chronic illness, failed careers. God permits or uses those trials to conform you in His image. We indeed are like metal. We do not change shape without heat and hammer.

2. God expects a response from us in the midst of trials. He wants us to humble ourselves and yield each moment to Him. He wants us to put His purposes ahead of our own selfish interests. Our initial reaction is, "I've got my rights!" He desires us to give up our rights and say, "Lord, I am willing to let You have Your way, even if it causes me discomfort or pain."

We must seek Jesus only! God is able to bring each of us to the end of our rope, to the point where our only alternative is to seek His help. When we cry out to Him, He answers. He will meet us at our point of need.

3. What does God promise to do? If we humble ourselves at His feet, He will lift us up, not in our time, but in His. He will demonstrate His power in our lives. Our weakness and dependence on Him give Him the opportunity to demonstrate His power in our lives. Our submission to His authority over us opens the door for His use of us. God promises to manifest His power in our lives, if we turn to Him in hope for deliverance.

4. What is the fruit of these trials? God uses trials to conform us in His image. Sanctification is the process of being slowly conformed to the image of Christ, day by day, until we are completed when we stand before the Savior. We do not conform ourselves. He conforms us, and suffering is His most effective tool. Four products of suffering that I have experienced are:

Suffering gives you a desire for heaven, a longing to be in God's presence.

Suffering makes you love God more.

Suffering makes you bold and takes away your fear of man.

Suffering takes away your fear of death.

5. We must seek an eternal perspective. God uses or permits suffering for our ultimate benefit. Through suffering we experience a fellowship with Christ that we would not have otherwise. We should view suffering as an interim process that leads to a much deeper relationship with Christ. Can we accept the hardship in exchange for the conforming work of Christ in our life?

Agony Relived—Again

It was Sunday evening at 11:00 three years to the month after Kelly died when we received another startling phone call. My niece had been injured in a snowmobile accident. She was on life-support systems and not expected to live. The shock and disbelief set in once again. How could this be? She was only twenty-four years old. I could feel the weakness as my strength began to fade. I became nauseous and fell into a stuporlike mood, not able to say much but quietly thinking about the agony my sister-in-law was experiencing. At approximately 1:30 A.M. we received the second call. My niece had died.

She was the middle of three children, same as our Kelly. She was named after me—Gia—not the same spelling as my name. She died five days before the anniversary of Kelly's death three years earlier. The parallels were amazing. Their personalities and spirits were identical. They both loved life, loved their families, loved their friends, and knew no strangers.

I am convinced there are special people whom our Lord calls home so that He can enjoy their presence. It had been just weeks earlier the Holy Spirit had led me to John 17:24 where Jesus prays His high priestly prayer. "Father, I want those you have given me to be with me where I am, and to see my glory, the glory you have given me because you loved me before the creation of the world."

There is only one answer why some live longer than others. There is work the Lord has for us. Lives we are to touch. Events in our lives that have not yet happened where we are to impact the lives of others.

For Kelly and Gia, their lives had been fulfilled, their missions completed. Their untimely deaths were the final act. Their deaths would have more impact on others than if they had lived. They were now to the point where their deaths would fulfill God's purposes more than their living.

I was convinced the Lord Jesus was returning soon. Gia's death was another sign for me, another of God's wake-up calls to this lost world, a call especially to family members who were continuing to reject God and His truths.

As Patty made phone calls to the rest of the family, I was again amazed at how people resist changes to their lives. I could feel the responses of some as I attempted to formulate in my mind the thoughts they were having. The unexpected death was not fitting into their plans for the coming week. Our lives are like a large locomotive going down the track of life. Once we are at cruising speed we don't want to stop. Once we have our destination identified, we don't like any track changes.

I could see God's purposes worked out as the days passed. People's hearts were softened. The reality of death was revealed to some who did not know it. Those who had never struggled with the issues of life and death were now forced to deal with them.

The stage was set for the funeral service. The hearts had been prepared to hear the messages, to hear the name of the Lord Jesus lifted up many times.

As I drove from Maryland to Ohio on Wednesday, I sought the Holy Spirit's leading. The funeral was to be the next day, Thursday. What could I do? What could I say? By the time I arrived in Akron that afternoon it was clear in my mind I wanted to participate in the funeral service. I wanted an opportunity to share the truth of life. The Holy Spirit had led my sister-in-law to the same conclusion, and she had already told the pastor I would most likely want to say something. The stage was set. The only thing remaining were the words. What would I say? I wanted to read the same passage from Revelation 21 that I read at my son's graveside. But, what else was I to say? I awoke at 2:30 Thursday morning and, for the next few hours, struggled as I sought the Holy Spirit's leading. Word after word was delivered, one small thought at a time was revealed as the puzzle was completed. Each Scripture passage was brought to my mind.

The last passage came to me as I sat in the chapel before the service. Turning the pages of my Bible, I found a piece of paper where I had written 2 Corinthians 1:3–5, which speaks of the suffering and comfort that flows into our lives: "Praise be to the God and Father of our Lord Jesus Christ, the Father of compassion and the God of all comfort, who comforts us in all our troubles, so that we can comfort those in any trouble with the comfort we ourselves have received from God. For just as the sufferings of Christ flow over into our lives, so also through Christ our comfort overflows."

Sitting there feeling the agony pressing on my heart, I thought of the comfort that is delivered when one turns to Christ. There and only there lies *true* comfort.

I was reminded my very survival was determined when I turned to Christ in my deepest despair. There was nothing Patty could say, nothing our pastor could say, nothing any friend could say that would comfort me. The only relief came from turning to Christ. The Holy Spirit is the only comforter in times of greatest trial.

The service started, and when my turn came, I began by speaking of my closeness to Gia. Since she had been named after me, I always felt a little piece of her was mine. I related how after Kelly died I knew the pain but also the comfort that comes by turning to Jesus. I read 2 Corinthians 1:3–5.

I talked about how special Gia was and how similar she was to Kelly. I read John 17:24, which tells how Christ longs for His children to be with Him. I quoted Hebrews 11:1: "Now faith is being sure of what we hope for and certain of what we do not see."

I spoke of Jesus' coming the first time as a lamb to sacrifice Himself for our sins and His coming again to estab-

130

lish His second kingdom. I read Revelation 21:1–7 and concluded in prayer. The two officiating pastors followed, and the whole service displayed itself as a beautiful picture.

Again I was reminded how God uses suffering as His greatest tool.

The next day while we were returning home, I thought about verse four in 2 Corinthians 1: ". . . so that we can comfort those in any trouble with the comfort we ourselves have received from God."

I said to Patty as we rode in the car, "I just had a scary thought. Did our son die so that we could comfort others?" Patty sat quietly and did not respond. She knew the pain I was experiencing at the moment. We had now grown to the point where we felt each other's pain without even exchanging words.

Encouragement from Kelly's Friends

Over the years since Kelly's death, his classmates have not stopped ministering to Patty and me. Each year on the anniversary of Kelly's death, they have sent us a card signed by each class member with flowers or another appropriate gift. What a comfort it is to know his friends have not forgotten him.

The pinnacle of their remembrance was their senior yearbook, in which they included a tribute to Kelly. Following are some excerpts.

I'll always remember his friendly attitude and smile, and
how he always said "hi" to me.

—Jodi

He always looked inside of people instead of at their
outward appearance.

—Jill

131

Kelly was always so giving. He was nice to me even when others were not.

—John

In seventh-grade English, I sat in front of him and we always compared our grades on our vocab tests. He was a great friend.

—Jeff

His smile could light up a room like no other. I never heard him make fun of anyone.

—Jason

Kelly was my best friend. I can remember weekend sleepovers at Kelly's. He had this really cool pond in his development and we would go fishing or ice skating there. Then seventh grade came when we were finally on the "big" campus. Kelly and I started carpooling together and we both played soccer that fall. I can still see him playing wing. However, on February 19, 1991, everything changed. Kelly suffered a cerebral hemorrhage and the Lord he loved called him home. In recent years, I have often wondered how great a soccer player Kelly would have become. Kelly, I just wanted to take this time to say thank you for the memories and to let you know that our little time together will forever be etched into my heart.

—Timothy

The remembrance is painful, but the recognition is consoling and touches our hearts.

At the graduation ceremony, five years and four months after our son's death, one of his classmates gave a brief remembrance of Kelly and presented us with a red graduation cap adorned with a small bouquet of miniature red roses.

I am convinced just as God has changed my life through Kelly's death, so He has changed the lives of each of these young women and men. And so it is, when a stone drops into water, the ripple effect is in motion; likewise God continues to use the events in our lives to not only change us but also those around us, as we touch the lives of each other.

Becoming a Shepherd

People who endure suffering are uniquely equipped to be shepherds. Dr. Larry Crabb reveals this when he writes: "Shepherds . . . have a knack for surfacing both deeply hidden ugliness without becoming disdainful and terrifying pain without collapsing. This sort of wisdom and gentle discernment is given only to saints who seek God through the worst anguish and who learn to yield cherished dreams to God's purposes."[1]

Shepherds are not born. They are the products of God's conforming hand. As a result of enduring my son's death I have found that God has softened my heart and made me much more empathetic to others' situations. I am no longer known as the "ice man." I have sensitivity and a willingness to listen to others while being able to offer an encouraging word. Furthermore, there is very little that shocks me. Events that would have previously caused me great difficulty are no longer as stressful. I am no longer surprised by the agony of life; I have grown to expect trial and tribulation. These are useful attributes when confronted with people's sinful behavior in a counseling situation.

Dr. Crabb identifies the process God uses to develop us into shepherds. First, we must seek God. In the midst of suffering we must turn to God for strength, mercy, and direction. We must reach out to Him, ask Him to take our hand and lead us through the trial. Without God's direction we will flounder in the muck and become bitter with the futility of our progress.

Second, we must yield our dreams to Him. I have repeated time and time again that life has not turned out the way I wanted it. My dreams have not been realized. However, by God's grace I have accepted this, and God has shown me that I must be willing to set my dreams aside and accept His purposes for my life and my family. This is the act of submission and the sacrificing of our wills. We cannot truly be His servants if we are following our own agenda. We cannot yield our life to Him if we are seeking to fulfill our own plan. God is able to strip the desire for control from us through the fire of trial and tribulation. In the midst of suffering God brings us to the point where we give up our desire for control. The more we fight Him and resist His conforming hand the longer the healing process takes. We must get to the point where we accept our tragedy. God permitted it, and I must accept it and look to Him to use it to conform me in His image.

God's perfect plan is being worked out; I can see evidence as I look back at the past. God is indeed in control of all things!

Oh, dear Lord, how my value system has changed with the passing of my son. My mind and emotions have been recalibrated, readjusted by Your fingertips gently touching my life. It is as if I have come from a different world as I talk to and observe others. How insignificant are the things that bother so many.

Dear Lord, You have shown me that to die is gain. And therefore, death, which poses as man's greatest fear, has lost its power over me and offers no threat. Life shall be truly different from this point on as I yield my mind and heart to Your control. You have told us that this life is but a pale reflection of that to come, and so I wait Your calling with anticipation.

June 13

Chapter 9

Lessons Learned

A Spiritual Relationship with Christ

The greatest lesson I have learned is God desires each of His children to have a single-minded, passionate relationship with Jesus Christ. Christ seeks our undivided and devoted love above all else. There is to be nothing that stands between Christ and me, nothing I value more—not my wife, not my children, not my job, not my money, not my hobby. Nothing in this world is to be more important than my relationship with Jesus Christ.

Being Filled with Christ

We read in the Gospel of Mark: "Love the Lord your God with all your heart and with all your soul and with all your mind and with all your strength" (12:30). The love of Christ is to fill every crevice in my body and soul. There are to be no voids and no areas to which Christ is not permitted. There are to be no "out of bounds" and no "no trespassing" signs to restrict Christ's access to my mind and soul. Christ desires to be complete master of each element of my very being.

"If anyone comes to me and does not hate his father and mother, his wife and children, his brothers and sisters— yes, even his own life—he cannot be my disciple" (Luke 14:26). Christ does not expect me to hate my family. He uses this statement in Luke 14 to illustrate the devotion He requires. My love of Christ is to be the dominating love in my life. My love for Christ is to be so consuming that on a relative scale it is as if I hated my family. There is to be no person in my life whom I love more than Jesus Christ, not my spouse, not my children, and not even myself.

This single-minded, passionate love is exemplified by Jesus when He clears the temple in John 2. In this act Jesus demonstrates His love for the Father and the Father's house. The disciples then remembered that it was written, "Zeal for your house will consume me" (John 2:17). Zeal and this single-minded love are one and the same.

Bishop J. C. Ryle drew a vivid description of zeal when he wrote:

> A zealous man in religion is pre-eminently a man of one thing. It is not enough to say that he is earnest, hearty, uncompromising, thorough-going, whole-hearted, fervent in spirit. He only sees one thing, he cares for one thing, he lives for one thing, he is swallowed up in one thing; and that one thing is to please God. Whether he lives, or whether he dies—whether he has health, or whether he has sickness— whether he is rich, or whether he is poor—whether he pleases man, or whether he gives offence—whether he is thought wise, or whether he is thought foolish—whether he gets blame, or whether he get praise—whether he gets honour, or whether he gets shame—for all this the zealous man cares nothing at all. He burns for one thing; and that one thing is to please God, and to advance God's glory. If he is consumed in the very burning, he cares not for it—he is

content. He feels that, like a lamp, he is made to burn; and if consumed in burning, he has but done the work for which God appointed him. Such a one will always find a sphere for his zeal. If he cannot preach, work, and give money, he will cry, and sigh, and pray. . . . If he cannot fight in the valley with Joshua, he will do the work of Moses, Aaron, and Hur, on the hill [Exodus 17:9–13]. If he is cut off from working himself, he will give the Lord no rest till help is raised up from another quarter, and the work is done.[1]

I believe my relationship with Christ is to be a consuming fire within me, a fire characterized by those zealous feelings that will not permit any other relationship to exist or interfere with my relationship with Him. The amazing thing is this devotion to Him does not detract from the love for others. The more we love Jesus the more love abounds in our being and the more capable we are of loving.

Being Used by God

Oswald Chambers states this passionate relationship must exist before we can be used by God for His work. He said, "Our Lord implies that the only men and women He will use in His building enterprises are those who love Him personally, passionately, and devotedly beyond any of the closest ties on earth."[2]

God will not use me for His work unless my love for Christ exceeds all other loves.

As I have worked through my son's death, God has nurtured and grown within me a love for Christ that far exceeds what existed in my heart before my son's death. I believe this is a fruit of the humbling process. In desperation as I have reached out to Him, He has filled my heart with an abounding love for Him. This abounding love for Christ has in no way diminished my love for my wife and remaining children. It is as if my heart has grown larger, becoming more compassionate and more loving than ever before. This is a work of the Spirit, not of me. I was not born with a caring nature. My nature has always been more independent and introvert. The Holy Spirit has changed my nature and molded me into a much more caring person.

I am convinced there are times when God immerses us in tribulation for the purpose of further developing our relationship with Him. If God desires to use me, He will prepare me for the mission. Oswald Chambers spoke about God coming in clouds, clouds of trial: "Is there anyone save Jesus only in your cloud? If so, it will get darker; you must get to the place where there is no one any more save Jesus only."[3]

We frequently strive to handle problems by ourselves. This is especially true of routine, daily trials common to most people. However, as the trials of life become more difficult, we begin to realize our inadequacies. Pride plays a major role in our inability to see those inadequacies and can be a true barrier. Furthermore, our culture teaches and encourages a self-sufficient attitude. I can clearly see this in my own life. Prior to Kelly's death, I was a self-sufficient person, needing very little from anyone else and believing that I could handle most anything. My son's death destroyed my self-sufficiency. I now see how God uses clouds and how He controls the severity of the storm. If God desires to develop in me a dependency on Him, He can create or permit the circumstances in my life that will accomplish the desired results. Need I wait for Him or can I yield control to Him without experiencing the trauma?

Even as I yield my being to Him, there are no guarantees trial and tribulations will cease. There are a multitude of reasons why we suffer and humbling me is only one of those reasons.

I am to love Jesus first and foremost. Christ asks, "Do you truly love me . . . ? . . . Feed my lambs. . . . Take care of my sheep" (John 21:15–17). In other words, "Love Me first; then do My work as an expression of your love for Me."

Feeding the lambs and taking care of the sheep are the outgrowth of my love for Christ. If I place the work ahead of the relationship or if I sacrifice the relationship for the work, the work becomes laborious and unmeaningful.

Oftentimes I am diverted away from my relationship with Christ by the very work I seek to accomplish for Him. Satan uses my very nature, which is to place the work ahead of my relationship with Christ, to draw me away from the relationship. I am further misled by the very thoughts of the importance of the work. I frequently think, *How can my relationship with Christ not be right when I am accomplishing so much for Him?* This is indeed another of Satan's lies, and it is the very issue at the heart of an incident in Luke 10. Jesus is visiting at the home of Martha and Mary. Martha is in the kitchen preparing the meal while Mary is spending time with Jesus. Martha, who is busily doing the work, becomes irritated by Mary's failure to help and asks Jesus to reprimand her sister. Jesus' response is: "Mary has chosen what is better, and it will not be taken away from her" (Luke 10:42).

Jesus points out to Martha that Mary's desire to spend time with Him is more important than the labor in the kitchen. The kitchen labor was necessary if Christ and the others were to eat; however, time with Christ was more important and took precedence over all other endeavors.

Maintaining the Relationship through Prayer

How easily I am distracted from my relationship with Christ even by the very work I seek to do for Him. In fact, it has been my experience, working *for* Him requires far less effort than maintaining a relationship *with* Him. I have found it much easier to teach a Sunday school class, lead a Bible study, or help a fellow Christian than to sit down for a quiet time of prayer and meditation with my Lord Jesus Christ. I would rather get up and do something than sit and wait for His direction. This is one reason I am not inclined to pray.

Another reason is the barrier of self-sufficiency. There is a direct correlation between my sense of self-sufficiency and the amount of prayer in my life. The more self-sufficient I am, the less I need God and His intervention. Conversely, the more humble and broken I am, the more inclined I am to seek God's direction.

Arthur W. Pink describes prayer thus: "The prevailing idea seems to be, that I come to God and ask Him for something that I want, and that I expect Him to give me that which I have asked. But this is a most dishonoring and degrading conception. The popular belief reduces God to a servant, our servant doing our bidding, performing our pleasure, granting our desires. No; prayer is a coming to God, telling Him my need, committing my way unto the Lord, and leaving Him to deal with it as seemeth Him best." Pink further says, "Prayer is taking an attitude of dependency upon God."[4]

Oswald Chambers said, "God does not exist to answer our prayers, but by our prayers we come to discern the mind of God."[5] Prayer is the means by which our minds and thoughts are conformed to God's mind. We do not change God's mind, He changes our minds. Prayer is not to be me submitting my "to do list" to God.

Prayer is meant to be a state of being, a continual communing with our Lord. A moment by moment dialogue with Him, an exchanging of ideas, and the maintaining of a relationship. I am convinced this relationship cannot be maintained outside of prayer. Prayer is the primary means, if not the sole means, of communicating with Christ.

Chambers said, "Prayer is getting ourselves attuned to God, not getting God attuned to us. It is developing the life of God in us."[6] I admit my most frequent prayers are petitions where I need God to meet a need or intervene. I spend little time praising Him and even less time listening for His small still voice. I realize if my mind is to be conformed to His mind, I must spend less time talking and more time meditating and listening. I must view prayer as God's opportunity to change my mind and give me direction. Yet, I frequently spend 80 percent of my prayer time giving Him direction and 20 percent receiving direction and instruction when in fact it must be the opposite.

Reordering Our Behavior

Oswald Chambers clearly emphasized the proper perspective when he said, "The main thing about Christianity is not the work we do, but the relationship we maintain."[7]

The realization of this perspective requires a shift in focus and will. We are a works-oriented people and therefore to shift from a works orientation to a relationship orientation requires a reordering of our behavior and thoughts. Development of the relationship necessitates putting our actions aside and spending quiet time in prayer. We must value our time with Christ more than we value our accomplishments for Him. This is difficult because we get no recognition from this world for spending time with Him yet we do get worldly recognition for our accomplishments. Our fellow believers may even be part of this problem because of their recognition of our accomplishments for God's kingdom. I am convinced Christ much prefers us spending time with Him rather than doing some great work for Him.

Utter dependence is the only doorway through which the Holy Spirit works. Any sense of self-sufficiency becomes a barrier in God's use of me. God uses only broken people to accomplish His work.

Even though years previously I had turned my life over to Christ and submitted myself to His authority over me, I had not truly been broken until I experienced the death of my son. My first reaction to Kelly's death was, "This is not fair!" I felt as if my rights had been violated. However, as I continued to wrestle with God over these issues, He began to show me that I really have no rights; He is in control. It was His desire that I submit to Him totally and say, "Lord, I am willing to be used by You. Do with me as You please."

Yet, how do I apply this principle as I live out each day? I must begin each day mindful of my desire and willing to let Him have His way with me. This principle will not be accomplished if I do not have a purposeful intent. My nature will not take me down this path. Therefore, I must ask the Spirit to intercede. This requires asking God to give me strength to do what I cannot do. If I let my nature lead, I will spend the day protecting my rights and interests.

If God has permitted Kelly's death, can I yield control to Him if He permits the death of my second son? If God permits me to lose my job, can I submit? If God lets me get cancer, can I yield to Him or would I revolt in anger?

I must realize there is nothing within me that makes me useful to God. If I have any feeling of bringing something to the table, then I am in immediate interference with God's plan. I must see myself as an empty carcass, useful to God only after He has filled it with His wisdom and energy.

God must humble me before He can use me. How often my attitude has been, "Let me show you, God, what I can do for you." I have realized how wrong this is. He is much more inclined to use me when I admit in humility I have nothing useful for Him. When I am incapable of doing the job and ask Him to give me the strength, then I am equipped to be used by Him.

I have no rights to my dreams or desires. I must be willing to give up my rights so that the Father's purposes may be realized in and through me. Demanding "my rights" is the manifestation of selfishness within my soul. Often in hard-nosed style I have fought to maintain my rights, failing to submit to the other individual, failing to give up the ground I was holding onto so tightly. I have learned that I own nothing. Everything I have belongs to God and has been given to me by Him. He therefore has complete freedom to retrieve anything at His leisure and to refrain from giving me anything I desire.

It is okay to have dreams and desires; however, when my dreams deviate from God's plan, I need to realize I have no right to demand that things be my way. Since I have been purchased by Christ, He has control of my life, and I must sacrifice my rights to His dominion. Once I have yielded my being to Him, my dreams are secondary to His plan for my life. I am then in full submission to Him. He has authority over my family, my job, all my activities, and everything I do and think. He is the master and my greatest desire is to please Him, even when it requires giving up my desires and dreams. I must yield everything to Him.

Achieving Brokenness through Suffering

Suffering is God's most effective tool for conforming us to the image of Jesus Christ. God puts His workers through the refining fire; the greater the mission, the hotter the fire.

Nothing changes a person more quickly or more completely than suffering. Nothing alters one's perspective or values faster than suffering. Complete value systems can be changed in moments when one becomes immersed in suffering.

I know of no man, other than Christ, who was used more by God than the apostle Paul. Yet, as I read Paul's letters, I become aware that no man other than Jesus Christ suffered more than the apostle Paul.

I have worked much harder, been in prison more frequently, been flogged more severely, and been exposed to death again and again. Five times I received from the Jews the forty lashes minus one. Three times I was beaten with rods, once I was stoned, three times I was shipwrecked, I spent a night and a day in the open sea, I have been constantly on the move. I have been in danger from rivers, in danger from bandits, in danger from my own countrymen, in danger from Gentiles; in danger in the city, in danger in the country, in danger at sea; and in danger from false brothers. I have labored and toiled and have often gone without sleep; I have known hunger and thirst and have often gone without food; I have been cold and naked.

2 Corinthians 11:23–27

None of us, regardless of our infirmities, can claim the suffering the apostle Paul experienced. This relationship between suffering and the conforming hand of God existed for the other disciples as well and was also evident in the lives of other great Christians in history. Those who have been used in the greatest manner by God have also endured the greatest hardships.

Although the connection between suffering and being used of God was hidden from me before my son died, it seems so evident now. God does not require suffering, but He does require brokenness, and suffering is the predominant means of achieving brokenness. When we are not broken, our nature dictates that we serve ourselves. When we are not broken, our wills are in conflict with God's will. But when we are broken, we are prepared to be used of God.

A Physical Relationship with Christ

I am convinced Jesus wants me to be with Him. I am not referring to a spiritual relationship, which indeed He desires; I am referring to being in His physical presence.

Jesus said, "Father, I want those you have given me to be with me where I am, and to see my glory" (John 17:24).

Christ dwells in heaven; His glory is in heaven. Therefore, when He says He wants me to be with Him and to see His glory, this can only be accomplished in heaven. The Lord Jesus Christ wants His people to be with Him in heaven. I take that literally, meaning now. His desire is that all His children be with Him in heaven NOW.

Longing for Heaven

I believe we are to desire to be with Him. "We are confident, I say, and would prefer to be away from the body and at home with the Lord" (2 Cor. 5:8). "Away from the body" is to have experienced death and to be in a spiritual form. "At home with the Lord" is to be in heaven. So the apostle Paul would encourage each of us to desire to die and be in heaven. Is that your desire? If God gave you a choice today to leave this earth, die, and depart to heaven, would you go?

He wants us to realize earth is not our home: "They are not of the world, even as I am not of it" (John 17:16).

An insightful question is, "Do I consider earth my home or do I consider heaven my home?" I am not talking intellectually but practically. Where do I prefer to be now? God wants me to realize heaven is my home. I find comfort in these passages:

> No eye has seen,
>   no ear has heard,
>   no mind has conceived
>   what God has prepared for those who love him.
>
> 1 Corinthians 2:9

> Rejoice and be glad, because great is your reward in heaven.
>
> Matthew 5:12

Now is your time of grief, but I will see you again and you
will rejoice, and no one will take away your joy.

John 16:22

Do I have a longing for heaven? Would I go there today
if I could?

There is a song that captures the essence of the relationship with Jesus and the desire to be with Him. The
stanzas to which I relate are:

> Let me know the kisses of your mouth.
> Let me feel your warm embrace.
> Let me smell the fragrance of your touch.
> Let me see your lovely face.
> Take me away with you.
> Even so, Lord, come.
> I love you, Lord.
> I love you more than life.[8]

I have thought about these issues many times and continue to do so frequently. I do believe the Lord Jesus wants
me to long to be in His physical presence. Some would say,
but what about your wife and remaining children? Do you
long to be separated from them? No, I do not long to be
separated from my wife and remaining children; however,
I do believe God would take care of them and use my death
in a mighty way to continue changing them if He were to
take me. There is no question, the ideal is for Christ to
return and establish His kingdom. Then I am with Christ,
with my departed son, Kelly, and with my wife and remaining children all at the same time. This is indeed the best
of all.

If He wants me to be with Him and I want to be with Him,
why am I not called home today? There is one reason. He
has work for me to do. "So we make it our goal to please
him, whether we are at home in the body or away from it"
(2 Cor. 5:9).

I am convinced if you are a child of God, there is one reason you are not now in heaven and that is because God has work for you to do. God's plan for you has not been completed. Once His plan has been completed you shall depart.

Measuring Time

I have realized life is so short; even as David said, "Show me, O LORD, my life's end and the number of my days; let me know how fleeting is my life. You have made my days a mere handbreadth; the span of my years is as nothing before you. Each man's life is but a breath" (Ps. 39:4–5). Matthew Henry eloquently commented on this passage when he said, "We need no rod, no pole, no measuring line, wherewith to take the dimension of our days, nor any skill in arithmetic wherewith to compute the number of them. No; we have the standard of them at our fingers' end, and there is no multiplication of it; it is but one hand-breadth in all. Our time is short, and God has made it so."[9]

I have accepted the alien status David described in the Psalms. "Hear my prayer, O LORD, listen to my cry for help; be not deaf to my weeping. For I dwell with you as an alien, a stranger, as all my fathers were. Look away from me, that I may rejoice again before I depart and am no more" (Ps. 39:12–13). Regarding this passage Matthew Henry's comments were, "David's afflictions had helped to wean him from the world and to take his affections off from it. Now he began, more than ever, to look upon himself as a stranger and sojourner here, like all his fathers, not at home in this world, but traveling through it to another, to a better, and would never reckon himself at home till he came to heaven."[10]

Since Kelly's death I have truly come to realize I am in this world but not of this world. Just as the psalmist describes, I am an alien or sojourner who seeks to go home. The chains holding me down to this world have been unbolted or cut. I am no longer counting on this life to satisfy my deepest longings. I am like a helium-filled balloon that has been cut loose and is quickly ascending to a higher world. My focus has turned from this life to the next.

God's Grace

Many have said, "I could not endure losing my child." I have found God gives the grace we need at the moment we need it, not one second too soon and not one second too late. At the right moment He delivers.

Prior to a trial, we do not possess the strength or the wherewithal to endure or overcome it. It is not within us. It is God's desire that we turn to Him in times of trial, and it is His promise to deliver us at His appointed time. This is indeed what He does. He will not deliver us when we desire, and He will not deliver us before the appointed time. However, at precisely the right moment as determined by God, He will provide the strength to endure or overcome the current tribulation, if we are willing to lean into the pain with Him. If we turn to Him and trust in His deliverance, He will not fail us.

If there is no need for deliverance, there is no need for grace. If grace were delivered before the right moment, it would be as pouring out a glass of water on the ground during a rainstorm. It would go unnoticed. However, if the glass is poured out on the parched ground during a drought, then it is most appreciated. So indeed is God's grace; it is not delivered until it is needed.

Likewise, God only delivers a portioned dose. He only gives the grace needed for the moment. He does not give the grace needed for tomorrow. This is why the burden of tomorrow, anticipated today, seems overwhelming. We do not have the grace today to overcome tomorrow's trial.

In Webster's Ninth New Collegiate Dictionary, we find that fortitude is "strength of mind that enables a person to encounter danger or bear pain or adversity with courage." This is a most appropriate description of what we need in the midst of trial and tribulation. God has the power by His grace to give us the fortitude to see life through this day and to help us "press on" when we feel mired in despair. We may feel the pain is too great to bear, but God is able to supply the fortitude which we cannot muster within ourselves. By His grace He will provide the faith to believe when we can do nothing but trust Him. "And the God of all grace, who called you to his eternal glory in Christ, after you have suffered a little while, will himself restore you and make you strong, firm and steadfast" (1 Peter 5:10).

Childlike Trust

God wants me to trust Him like a little child trusts his father. "I tell you the truth, unless you change and become like little children, you will never enter the kingdom of heaven" (Matt. 18:3).

Can I trust Christ to take care of my spouse and children if He takes me home to be with Him? Can I have the faith of the child who would go anywhere holding the hand of the loving father and mother? Can I follow Christ and rely on Him to deliver me from any and every situation?

Every believer will one day come to the point where there is nothing left but to trust God. It may be the day before you go into surgery when you have no assurance of survival. At that moment there is nothing you can do. You are at the mercy of the doctor. Your only alternative is to trust God, believing He is in control of the eternal plan for your life. Can you and will you trust Him?

> In him we were also chosen, having been predestined according to the plan of him who works out everything in conformance with the purpose of his will, in order that we, who were the first to hope in Christ, might be for the praise of his glory.
>
> Ephesians 1:11–12

The apostle Paul tells us we have been "predestined according to the plan." God has a plan for each one of us. Can I believe God's plan, not my plan, is being executed in my life?

Paul further tells us "the plan" is in "conformance with the purpose of his will." God's plan which He is executing in my life is in complete conformance with His will. Can I believe nothing happens outside of God's plan for me? Can I believe nothing happens God has not predestined before the beginning of time?

Paul concludes by telling us the plan, which is in conformance with God's purposes, is ultimately for the "praise of his glory." My life, which God has predestined or planned out before time, will give praise to God. All my ups and downs, all my failures and successes, all my trials and tribulations have been foreordained and will give praise to God. Can I believe this is so? Will I trust in Him to fulfill this promise? This is the bottom line.

Ask God to give you the faith to believe. Trust in Him to work it all out according to His perfect plan for you.

This childlike trust was displayed in my good friend, David Saadeh, as he was dying from a brain tumor. When I visited Dave, he repeated these questions, "Is God sovereign? Can I trust Him?" He needed to know that God was in control and that God would take care of his family. He wanted to trust in God's perfect plan even though God's plan was turning out differently than his. Each time I visited Dave I told him, "You are the blessed one, for through your suffering you are being conformed more and more in the image of the Lord Jesus." Dave fought the good fight and finished the race yielding his dreams and trusting in his Lord. This is the battle each of us must wage.

I conclude with this quote from Larry Crabb: "Our fiercest battles are fought when we seek with all our heart to trust God so fully that we see every misfortune as something he permits and wants to use, to know him so richly that we turn to no one and nothing else to experience what our souls long to enjoy, to love him so completely and with such consuming passion that we hate anything that comes between us and eagerly give it up."[11]

Oh, dear Lord, how can some deny Your existence or worse yet, seem to ignore it? Need we only briefly measure the things we cannot understand. How large is the universe? Where does it end? Consider the complexity of the human body. Could it happen by accident? Did it evolve over a period of time or one day appear by a chance meeting of molecules?

Lord, there is too much left unexplained even by the most intelligent of people.

So, dear Lord, if this logic drives one to accept Your existence, why do we then fear death and refuse to discuss or even think of the life after? We only seem to focus on the now. We deny that we have grown older. We block out that we too will some day die and face the judgment of our creator.

Dear Lord, this life seems to me but a trial run, a practice session for the "real" life that follows. How can a few years measure up to infinity?

June 13

Notes

Chapter 4

1. Oswald Chambers, *My Utmost for His Highest* (Grand Rapids: Discovery House Publishers [Oswald Chambers Publications Assn., Ltd. Original edition copyright 1935 by Dodd, Mead, & Co.]), May 5.
2. Wayne Watson, *Home Free*, Word Music and Material Music/ASCAP, 1990.
3. Henry H. Halley, *Halley's Bible Handbook* (Grand Rapids: Zondervan, 1965), 373.

Chapter 5

1. Chambers, *My Utmost for His Highest*, November 1.
2. C. S. Lewis, *The Problem of Pain* (New York: Macmillan, 1962), 110.
3. Ibid., 96.
4. M. R. DeHaan, *Broken Things, Why We Suffer* (Grand Rapids: Discovery House Publishers, 1988), 47.
5. Chambers, *My Utmost for His Highest*, August 4.
6. Lewis, *The Problem of Pain*, 97.
7. Ibid., 44.
8. Oswald Chambers, *If You Will Ask* (Grand Rapids: Discovery House Publishers, [1958 Oswald Chambers Publications Association Ltd.]), 77.

Chapter 6

1. Chambers, *My Utmost for His Highest*, November 1.
2. Larry Crabb, *Connecting* (Nashville: Word, 1997), 115.

Chapter 7

1. Crabb, *Connecting*, 150.

2. Don Moen, *I Want to Be Where You Are,* Integrity's Hosanna! Music/ASCAP, Integrity Music, Inc., 1989.

3. C. S. Lewis, *A Grief Observed* (New York: Bantam Books, 1961), 79–80.

Chapter 8

1. Crabb, *Connecting,* 82.

Chapter 9

1. Bishop J. C. Ryle, in J. I. Packer, *Knowing God* (Downers Grove: InterVarsity Press), 173.

2. Chambers, *My Utmost for His Highest,* May 7.

3. Chambers, *My Utmost for His Highest,* November 1.

4. Arthur W. Pink, *The Sovereignty of God* (Carlisle, Penn.: The Banner of Truth Trust, 1976), 118, 121.

5. Chambers, *If You Will Ask,* 50.

6. Ibid., 7.

7. Chambers, *My Utmost for His Highest,* August 4.

8. David Ruis, *True Love,* Mercy/Vineyard Publishing, 1994.

9. Matthew Henry, *Matthew Henry's Commentary,* vol. III (Old Tappan, N.J.: n.d.), 383.

10. Ibid., 385.

11. Crabb, *Connecting,* 150.